Disneyland Paris Travel Guide 2024

Plan Like a Pro, Play Like a Kid, Must-Dos and Don'ts, Chills and Eats: Your Enchantment Disneyland Paris Family Adventure

KYLE L. ANDERSON

Gain access to more books, scan this barcode!

About The Author

KYLE L. ANDERSON is not just an adventurer but also a storyteller, curator, and trusted companion on transformative journeys.

With a lifelong dedication to exploring the world's outer reaches, Kyle shares his discoveries driven by an insatiable wanderlust.

From embarking on his first solo expedition at 18 to traversing six continents, Kyle has ventured through deserts, climbed mountains, and explored extreme terrains.

Beyond ticking off bucket list destinations, Kyle values the connections formed with people and immersion in diverse cultures during his travels.

Committed to inspiring others, Kyle delves into travel writing and guidebook authorship, blending captivating storytelling with practical insights and meticulously researched information.

Kyle's guidebooks serve as passports to adventure, whether one seeks to trek through South American rainforests, explore Asian ruins, or embark on a road trip across the American West.

Encouraging travelers to venture off the beaten path and embrace the unknown, Kyle invites both seasoned adventurers and curious souls to embark on life-changing journeys.

With his passion for exploration, a wealth of knowledge, and unwavering dedication to adventure, **KYLE L. ANDERSON** stands ready to guide travelers toward fulfilling their travel aspirations.

About the Book

Experience the Enchantment of Disneyland Paris in 2024!

Welcome to your comprehensive guide to experience the enchantment of Disneyland Paris in 2024! This comprehensive travel guide is your one-stop shop for organizing an extraordinary experience that includes exhilarating rides, compelling performances, delectable cuisine, and treasured memories for the entire family.

Navigate the Magic With Ease:

Detailed Park Maps and Ride Guides: Immerse yourself in the marvel with clear, easy-to-follow park maps and ride descriptions. Discover wait times, FastPass+ tactics, and accessibility information for popular attractions like Space Mountain: Mission 2, Pirates of the Caribbean, and Big Thunder Mountain Railroad.

Unforgettable Experiences Beyond the Rides: Character Encounters & Show Schedules: Plan your days around spectacular parades, riveting stage plays, and meet-and-greets with your favorite Disney characters. This guide includes performance timings, character placements, and ideas for capturing those ideal moments.

Dining Adventures for Every Palate: Take a gourmet trip through a world of delights. Discover themed eateries, hidden gems, and the ideal setting for a quick lunch or a relaxing character dining experience. Detailed menus, allergy information, and cost-effective choices are all given.

Special Events & Seasonal Delights: Immerse yourself in the year's charm with enticing seasonal offers. This guide details interesting activities taking place throughout 2024, ranging from the heartwarming charm of Disney's Halloween Festival to the spectacular splendor of Disney's Christmas Season.

Travel Tips and Money-Saving Strategies:
Accommodation Options for Every Budget:
Discover the ideal location to stay, whether it's a lavish Disney hotel for optimum convenience or a lovely Parisian hotel for a taste of the local culture. This guide includes detailed reviews, price comparisons, and insider recommendations for getting the greatest bargains.

Expert Planning Strategies: Easily navigate transit alternatives, ticketing processes, and park logistics. Our travel experts provide helpful advice on how to make the most of your magical journey, save money on park staples, and maximize your time.

Bonus Content:
Hidden Gems & Secret Spots: Explore the park's lesser-known areas and uncover one-of-a-kind experiences that cannot be found elsewhere. From delightful stores to hidden Mickeys, this book reveals secrets that only genuine Disney enthusiasts know.

Planning for Families with Young Children: Ensure a stress-free vacation for the entire family by including sections on stroller rentals, infant care facilities, character dining experiences suitable for young children, and helpful hints for traversing the park with young adventurers.

Disneyland Paris is set to open in 2024! This thorough book will help you uncover a world of enchantment, adventure, and unforgettable experiences.

A few of the numerous books by KYLE L. ANDERSON

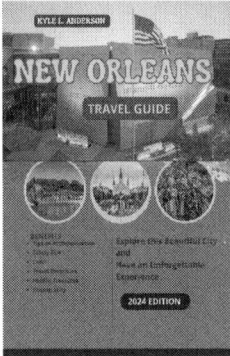

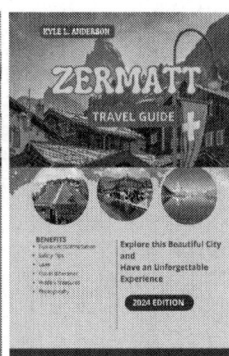

Table of Contents

Introduction

A Sparkling Welcome to Disneyland Paris:
Unveiling Magic
Step outside the everyday and into a world where
dreams may fly. Imagine wandering over
picturesque streets adorned with colorful buildings,
the air filled with contagious laughter from
children, and the enthralling tunes of classic Disney
films. Welcome to Disneyland Paris, where fairytales
come to life and every corner holds an exciting
surprise.

This travel guide is your golden ticket to discovering the wonders of Disneyland Paris. Disneyland Paris provides an extraordinary trip for all ages, whether you're a wide-eyed youngster discovering the marvel for the first time, a sentimental adult reliving cherished memories, or a couple looking for a romantic vacation.

Within these pages, you will go on an enthralling adventure. We'll look at how diligent planning delivers a flawless and memorable experience. We'll explore the vivid worlds of Disneyland Park and Walt Disney Studios Park, where classic attractions, spectacular shows, and unforgettable interactions with cherished characters await.

But Disneyland Paris offers more than simply thrilling rides and adrenaline-pumping roller coasters. We'll sample the wonderful treats served by the resort's many restaurants, which range from quaint cafés to world-class fine-dining experiences. You'll come across one-of-a-kind shopping options filled with antiques and mementos.

This journey goes past the park gates and into the enthralling city of Paris itself. We'll reveal day-trip itineraries that will allow you to see the famous Eiffel Tower, the breathtaking Louvre Museum, and the unmistakable charm of Parisian cafés and bistros.

So, pack your luggage, let your inner kid go, and be ready to be carried away by the enchantment of Disneyland Paris. This fascinating universe awaits, offering an extraordinary trip full of laughter, wonder, and life-long memories.

History and Overview

A Magical Legacy: Reflections on Disneyland Paris Disneyland Paris is more than simply a collection of rides and attractions; it is a destination rich in history and worldwide collaboration. Let's travel back in time to 1987, when the first magical seeds were planted.

Disneyland Paris was the result of years of planning and collaboration between the Walt Disney Company and the French government. The idea is to develop a European analog to the popular Disneyland in California, bringing the joy of Disney stories and characters to a new generation.

1992: Grand Opening and Early Years

On April 12th, 1992, the gates of Euro Disney, as it was originally known, opened for the first time. Imagine the thrill! A land brimming with historic castles, thrilling rides, and popular characters greeted eager visitors from throughout Europe. Euro Disneyland had one theme park (now called Disneyland Park) and multiple hotels, providing a full and comprehensive Disney experience.

Evolution & Adaptation

The early years were filled with both accomplishments and problems. Euro Disneyland required cultural adaptations because the word "Euro" had a different connotation for Europeans than Americans planned. In 1994, the resort's name was changed to Disneyland Paris, reflecting its genuine location and global appeal.

Disneyland Paris has grown and evolved. Walt Disney Studios Park debuted in 2002, bringing Hollywood's glitter and glamor, Pixar's imaginative realms, and Marvel's action-packed adventures to the resort.

The Legacy of Enchantment

Today, Disneyland Paris is the most popular tourist attraction in Europe. It's a location where families make enduring memories, couples rediscover their passion, and kids go on experiences that pique their interest. From the timeless charm of Disneyland Park to the cutting-edge thrills of Walt Disney Studios Park, the resort has something for everyone.

As you visit the parks, look for subtle allusions to European culture and architecture. Disneyland Paris stands out for its combination of Disney charm and European flair.

Now that you've discovered Disneyland Paris' interesting past, prepare to explore deeper! In the following chapter, we'll take a fantastic journey across the parks, discovering their enchanting areas, exhilarating rides, and unique character interactions.

Why Disneyland Paris in 2024?

But why would you select Disneyland Paris in 2024? Buckle up, fellow explorer, because this year promises to shine brighter than Cinderella's glass slipper!

A Spark of Something New: Disneyland Park will welcome the spectacular "Disney Symphony of Colours" in 2024. Prepare for vivid presentations and intriguing performances that will awaken your senses with a wonderful fusion of music, dance, and narrative. Imagine being carried away by a whirlwind of colors, leaving you singing Disney songs long after the final curtain falls.

Blooming with Enchantment: Springtime paints Disneyland Paris in a stunning color. Lush vegetation springs out, flowers blossom in a riot of hues, and the sun's soft warmth offers the ideal environment for exploration. Queues for rides feel shorter under beautiful blue skies, and evenings spent picnicking in the park with shimmering fairy lights overhead are memories you'll treasure for a lifetime.

Fewer Crowds, More Magic: 2024 falls perfectly between peak and shoulder seasons. The summer frenzy hasn't yet subsided, allowing you to tour the parks with greater ease and lower wait times. This means you'll have more time to soak up the enchantment, meet your favorite characters, and enjoy every exhilarating ride without feeling hurried.

Celebrating Special Occasions: Perhaps you're on honeymoon and want a bit of Parisian romanticism. Disneyland Paris in 2024 provides a pleasant retreat, with fireworks lighting up the night sky and cozy restaurants providing the ideal environment for a romantic encounter. Perhaps you are planning a family trip. This year's character dining experiences and magical parades will leave your children with sparkling eyes and memories to cherish for years to come.

But wait—there's more! The year 2024 promises to be filled with exciting Halloween and Christmas activities. Imagine frightening treats and glittering decorations for Halloween, or the uplifting splendor of a Parisian Christmas at Disneyland Park.

So, dear traveler, Disneyland Paris in 2024 is more than simply a vacation; it's a portal to a world filled with vivid colors, enthralling entertainment, and a hint of springtime enchantment. It's the perfect year to create your fairytale, full of joy, wonder, and memories that will last a lifetime.

Planning Your Dream Vacation

Ahoy, mates! Buckle your swashbuckling belts and go for Disneyland Paris, where a wave of wonder awaits. But, before you embark on this beautiful journey, a little preparation goes a long way toward ensuring a seamless and enjoyable experience. So, take your compass (or smartphone), and let's explore the thrilling world of trip planning!

Setting Sail for Adventure

Charting Your Course: Selecting the Perfect Dates

The first member of your planning team should be the calendar! Consider these criteria while selecting your vacation dates:

Seasonal Magic: Spring brings beautiful weather and blossoming flowers, while summer brings exciting entertainment and extended park hours. Autumn provides a pleasant environment and Halloween activities, while winter illuminates with Christmas wonderlands.

Crowd Control: Avoid busy seasons such as July and August if you desire shorter lines. The shoulder seasons (spring and fall) provide a nice blend of beautiful weather and moderate people.

Special Events: Do you crave the eerie thrills of Halloween or the warm warmth of a Parisian Christmas? Plan your trip around these engaging events to get an additional dose of enchantment.

Choosing Your Expedition Length:
How long will you stay? This is dependent on your sense of adventure!

A hectic weekend is ideal for thrill-seekers who want to try as many rides as possible. This fast-paced tour necessitates careful planning and optimizing park hours.

The pleasant middle (3–4 days): This allows you to take your time exploring both parks, dine with characters, and soak up the Disney atmosphere. An Enchanted Escape (5+ Days): Ideal for families with small children or those who want to fully immerse themselves in the enchantment. This program provides you with relaxation days, touring outside of the parks, and seeing unique shows. Setting sail with a budget in mind.

Every captain requires a treasure map, and yours is the budget! Disneyland Paris provides experiences for a wide range of budgets. Here's the breakdown:

Accommodation: Disney Hotels provides maximum convenience and immersive experiences, albeit at a premium price. Consider off-site hotels as a more cost-effective choice.

Park Tickets: Multi-day passes are more economical than single-day tickets. Examine many ticket options to determine the one that best fits your plan.

Food and Beverage: Dining plans are handy, but they may not meet everyone's needs. Consider bringing snacks and reusable water bottles to save some money.

Remember: Preparation is essential, especially during high seasons. Booking your accommodation and park tickets in advance might help you save money and get the dates you choose.

So, there you have it, mates! With careful preparation and a sprinkling of fairy dust, you can have a memorable journey at Disneyland Paris. Now, let us chart a plan for your next stop: selecting the ideal Disney hotel!

Accommodations Fit for Royalty: Selecting the Ideal Disney Hotel

Hi there, explorers! Now that you've set your path and secured your valuables (i.e., park tickets), it's time to select your ideal home away from home in Disneyland Paris. Disney has a fleet of spectacular hotels, each with a distinct theme, services, and closeness to the parks. So be ready to be wowed as we set sail across a sea of magical Disney lodgings!

Step into a fairy tale: Disney's Sequoia Lodge and Disneyland Hotel

If traditional Disney charm and a touch of rustic elegance appeal to you, choose Disney's Sequoia Lodge & Disneyland Hotel. Consider towering pine trees, toasty fireplaces, and a charming setting evocative of a big National Park lodge. These hotels are the nearest to Disneyland Park, making them ideal for visitors looking to make the most of their stay there. Character breakfasts, gorgeous pools, and wonderfully decorated rooms make these hotels ideal for families and Disney fans alike.

A World of Enchantment: Disney's Newport Bay Club & Hotel New York, The Art of Marvel

Calling all globetrotters and Marvel fans! Disney's Newport Bay Club transports you to a lovely New England-style seaside resort, replete with nautical elements and a cool ocean wind. For a bit of superhero swagger, check out nearby Hotel New York - The Art of Marvel, where you can live among your favorite Marvel superstars. Imagine themed rooms with classic artwork, character encounters with the Avengers, and a stunning pool designed like the iconic S.H.I.E.L.D. Helicarrier.

A Galactic Getaway at Disney's Disneyland Hotel and Disney's Hotel Cheyenne

Calling all space cadets! Disney's Disneyland Hotel brings you to a world of futuristic elegance, with elegant architecture and heavenly decorations creating an otherworldly environment. Consider looking at glittering constellations from your balcony or eating a galactic-themed supper. For a more affordable choice with a Wild West twist, Disney's Hotel Cheyenne provides a rootin' tootin' good time. Think dusty saloons, character breakfasts with Mickey and company dressed as cowboys, and a dynamic environment ideal for families with young explorers.

A Touch of Parisian Charm: Disney's Hotel Santa Fe and Disney's Davy Crockett Ranch
Do you want a dash of Parisian flair with your Disney magic? Disney's Hotel Santa Fe immerses guests in the brilliant colors and creative energy of Santa Fe, New Mexico. This beautiful hotel combines Southwestern flare with Disney fun. Disney's Davy Crockett Ranch offers a unique experience. Imagine rustic cottages tucked amid towering pines, replete with campfire activities and a laid-back ambiance ideal for families looking for a touch of nature to complement their Disney journey.

Choosing Your Best Fit

The best Disney Hotel depends on your budget, vacation style, and desired level of immersion. Consider the following variables while making your decision:

Theme and Ambiance: Do you want classic Disney charm, futuristic thrills, or a dash of Parisian flair?

Proximity to Parks: Do you value convenience and walking distance, or do you prefer a quick shuttle ride?

Amenities: Do you value character eating experiences, themed pools, or on-site restaurants?

Budget: Disney Hotels cater to a variety of budgets. Determine your lodging budget.

Remember that no matter what Disney Hotel you select, you will have an experience that is both magical and convenient. So, set sail and ready to be pampered like royalty at your preferred Disney destination!

Park Tickets and Passes: Planning Your Disney Adventure

Park Tickets and Passes: Planning Your Disney Adventure

Welcome back, intrepid travelers! Now that you've booked your swashbuckling hotel and set your park dates, it's time to explore the world of Disneyland Paris park tickets and passes. Consider this a treasure map to a world of exhilarating rides, enthralling performances, and unique character interactions.

A Sea of Ticket Options: Choosing the Perfect Fit

Disneyland Paris provides a selection of park tickets and passes to suit different budgets and vacation preferences. Here's a breakdown to assist you traverse this thrilling, but rather confusing territory:

Dated Tickets: Ideal for individuals with a specific agenda. These tickets provide entrance to either Disneyland Park, Walt Disney Studios Park, or both on a predetermined day.

27

Updated 1-Day Tickets provide flexibility for impulsive adventurers. These tickets are good for one year from the purchase date and provide entrance to any park on any non-blackout day.

Updated Multi-Day Tickets: The ticket to experiencing numerous days of enchantment. Choose between two, three, four, or even a fantastic five-day pass! These tickets provide the best value and are great for families or anyone planning a longer stay.

Consider "Plus" Options to Supercharge Your Adventure

Thinking about enhancing your experience with a little more pixie dust? Consider the following add-on options:

Disney Premier Access: This service allows you to avoid the wait at select high-demand attractions, saving you time and optimizing your park experience.

Disney PhotoPass+: Keep all of your amazing moments with unlimited digital downloads of

Disney PhotoPass images shot by professional photographers around the parks.

Important Tip to Remember:
Advanced booking is key: Booking your park tickets ahead of time is especially important during high seasons.
Compare Prices: Prices vary depending on the season, kind of ticket, and add-ons. Before you make a purchase, do some research and compare pricing.
Consider Age Requirements: Children under three years old can access the parks for free! Older children's ticket fees vary according to their age. Remember that the optimal ticket selection is based on your specific needs and preferences. Consider your budget, preferred amount of flexibility, and length of stay while making your selection.

With this treasure map in hand, you'll be able to easily navigate the world of Disneyland Paris park tickets and passes. Prepare to set sail for a voyage full of limitless thrills and amazing adventures!

Important Travel Tips: From Visas to Packing Must-Haves

Ahoy, mates! We've booked our ship (hotel) and planned our itinerary (dates and tickets), and now it's time to stuff the crow's nest (pack your luggage) for your magical trip to Disneyland Paris! But, before you set off, here is some crucial travel advice to ensure smooth sailing and make the most of your vacation.

Visas and Documents:
Visa Requirements: Most European residents do not need a visa to enter France. However, visitors from outside of Europe should verify visa requirements well in advance of their journey. Passport Power: Ensure that your passport is valid for at least 6 months beyond your trip dates.

Currency and Budgeting:
The Euro reigns supreme. France's official currency is the euro (EUR). Consider converting money before your trip or utilizing a travel-friendly credit card.
Budgeting for extras: Consider other expenditures like souvenirs, snacks, and meals that are not covered by any dining plans you may have purchased.

Packing for Adventure:
Dress for the Weather: The weather in Paris may be unpredictable. Pack adjustable layers, comfortable walking shoes, and a rain jacket or poncho.
Sun Smarties: Sunscreen, sunglasses, and a hat are necessary, especially during the summer months.
Must-Have Magic: Bring a refillable water bottle to remain hydrated all day, a portable phone charger to keep your gadget charged, and comfortable walking shoes to conquer those park miles.
Mickey Must-Haves: Pack Disney-themed apparel, especially for young explorers who will enjoy wearing their favorite characters.

Downloadable Treasures: Before your journey, download the official Disneyland Paris app. This useful program displays park maps, wait times, and entertainment schedules, and even allows you to mobile order meals!

Staying Connected:
International Roaming: Ask your mobile service provider about international roaming prices. Consider acquiring a local SIM card upon arrival.
Wi-Fi at Sea (and Land): Most Disney hotels have free Wi-Fi. The parks also offer specific Wi-Fi areas where you may stay connected.

Staying Healthy and Safe:
Pack Essentials: Bring basic medicines, allergy relief (if necessary), and other personal care products you may need.
Safety First: Disneyland Paris is extremely safe, but keep an eye on your possessions and little children, especially in crowded places.
Learning a Few French words: While English is frequently spoken at Disneyland Paris, learning a

few basic French words might help you have a better experience and enchant the locals.
Bonus Tip: If you plan on hiring a car during your vacation, learn about French traffic regulations and traditions first.

With these vital travel recommendations stowed away in your treasure chest, you'll be well on your way to a pleasant and spectacular vacation at Disneyland Paris. Batten down the hatches and prepare for an incredible journey full of fairy dust, exhilarating thrills, and magical memories!

Waltzing Through the Magic: Transportation to and around Disneyland Paris

Ahoy, mates! We secured our ship (hotel), plotted our path (dates and tickets), and filled the crow's nest (packed our luggage). Now it's time to set sail for the magical lands of Disneyland Paris! But before you can stroll through the mystical gates, you must first figure out how to get there. Fear not, intrepid visitors, for this chapter will serve as your trusted compass, leading you through airport alternatives, transfers, and navigating Disneyland Paris' efficient transportation system.

Landing Like A Fairytale: Airport Options in Paris

Paris has two major international airports: Charles de Gaulle Airport (CDG): CDG is the largest and busiest of the two airports, providing good connections to locations across the world. **Orly Airport(ORY):** ORY, a smaller and more manageable airport, is frequently utilized by budget airlines and may provide more easy connections for some passengers.

Transfers from the airport to the park are seamless.
Several handy travel choices will take you from the airport to your amazing Disneyland Paris journey.

Magical Shuttle: For a hassle-free experience, use the official Disneyland Paris shuttle service. This convenient and dependable alternative transports you straight from the airport to your accommodation.

Train Magic: The efficient TGV high-speed train network connects CDG and ORY airports to Marne-la-Vallée Chessy station, which is only a short walk or train ride from the Disneyland Paris parks.

Taxi Tales: Taxis are easily accessible at both airports. While handy, this method may be more expensive, particularly during busy hours.

Pro Tip: Consider getting a Paris Visite travel card before your trip. This simple pass provides unlimited access to public transit in Paris, including trains, buses, and the metro, possibly saving you money on airport transfers and visiting the city.

Once Upon A Magical Arrival:
When you arrive at your selected Disney Hotel, you will be met by the seamless wonder of Disneyland Paris. Most hotels have complimentary luggage transport services, letting you check in and immediately proceed to the park for your first taste of pixie dust.

Navigating the Enchanted Realm: Transportation at Disneyland Paris
You won't have to worry about transportation once you are in Disneyland Paris! The resort has a comfortable and fast internal transportation system, allowing you to tour both parks and travel around with ease.

Disneyland Railroad: Take a fanciful voyage on a lovely train, which provides a panoramic tour of the park and a delightful way to get from one land to another.

Main Street Vehicles: For a nostalgic touch to your park tour, board a historic horse-drawn trolley or omnibus and take a leisurely journey down Main Street, U.S.A.

Disney Buses: Free and convenient shuttle buses connect Disney Hotels to the parks and Disney Village, allowing for simple mobility around the resort.

Shank's Mare (Walking): Never underestimate the strength of your own two feet! Disneyland Paris is meant to be pedestrian-friendly, so strolling allows you to fully immerse yourself in the wonderful ambiance and hidden intricacies of the parks.

A final word on transportation:

Getting to and around Disneyland Paris is easy regardless of the method of transportation. With easy airport connections, a beautiful internal system, and the option of exploring on foot, you'll be waltzing through the magic in no time. So saddle up, mates, and prepare for an incredible adventure to a world where dreams may fly!

Navigating the City of Lights: Exploring Paris Beyond the Park

Ahoy, mates! While Disneyland Paris provides a mesmerizing realm of fantasy, don't overlook the wonders that lie outside the park gates! Paris, the City of Lights, entices visitors with its renowned sites, rich history, and unmistakable charm. So, set sail for an intriguing excursion beyond the parks and explore the enchantment that awaits you in this majestic city.

Day trips to iconic landmarks:
Eiffel Tower: No vacation to Paris is complete without climbing the Eiffel Tower. Soar to the top for spectacular panoramic views of the city, or have a romantic meal at the Jules Verne restaurant, perched high above the Paris skyline.
The Louvre, home to the Mona Lisa and numerous other creative treasures, is a treasure trove for art lovers. Wander through vast halls, admire antique relics, and immerse yourself in the splendor of human invention.
Notre Dame Cathedral: This stunning specimen of Gothic architecture is a must-see. Explore the

beautiful carvings and stained glass windows, and take in the awe-inspiring ambiance of this historic relic.

The Arc de Triomphe, which commemorates French conquests, stands as a towering emblem of French pride. Climb to the summit for panoramic views of the Champs-Élysées, or see the changing of the guard ceremony.

Beyond the Tourism Trail:
Paris has hidden beauties waiting to be uncovered.

Montmartre: Discover the picturesque hilltop area of Montmartre, formerly a sanctuary for artists such as Picasso. Wander through cobblestone alleyways, see the Sacré-Coeur Basilica, and take in the bohemian vibe.

Immerse yourself in the fashionable Marais area, which is known for its elegant boutiques, art galleries, and lively cafes. People watch in gorgeous squares or eat a tasty lunch at a nearby café.

Latin Quarter: Explore the ancient Latin Quarter, which is filled with prestigious colleges, busy bookstores, and a young spirit. Explore the

Pantheon, take a stroll through the lovely Jardin du Luxembourg, or get lost in the labyrinthine lanes of this fascinating area.

Parisian Culinary Adventure:
Paris is a sanctuary for foodies! Step outside the parks and enjoy the city's gastronomic delights:

French Bistros: Enjoy traditional French food in a quaint cafe environment. Imagine creamy onion soup, succulent steak frites, and luscious desserts. Embrace the Parisian cafe culture. Sip a café au lait, have a pain au chocolat, and watch the world go by from a lovely curbside patio.
Michelin-Starred Splendor: For an outstanding experience, dine at a Michelin-starred restaurant. Prepare to be blown away by creative food and superb service.
Pro Tip: Get a Paris Museum Pass for cheap admission to several of the city's best sites, including the Louvre and the Musee d'Orsay.

Parisian Fairytale:
Exploring Paris allows you to experience a distinct type of magic. From famous buildings to attractive neighborhoods and scrumptious food, the City of Lights provides an amazing trip to match the magic of Disneyland Paris. So, take sail beyond the park gates and experience the wonders that await you in this great city!

Recommended Travel Itineraries for your Disneyland Paris adventure

This section offers a template for creating your ideal Disneyland Paris schedule, appealing to a variety of interests and travel types. Consider these options as a starting point, and feel free to tailor them to your group's tastes, preferred speed, and duration of stay.

Itinerary 1: Conquer the Classics (1 Day)
This schedule is suitable for first-time tourists or those with limited time who wish to see the most popular sights. Prepare for some wait times, particularly during busy seasons.

Morning:

Arrive at the park's opening and proceed right to a popular attraction like Hyperspace Mountain: Mission 2 or Big Thunder Mountain Railroad.

Use FastPass+ wisely for popular rides such as Pirates of the Caribbean Indiana Jones and the Temple of Peril.

Explore Adventureland, where you may experience the thrills of Indiana Jones and the Temple of Peril and cruise the exotic rivers of Pirates of the Caribbean.

Afternoon:

Visit Fantasyland for a nostalgic trip on Peter Pan's Flight and a fanciful adventure through Pinocchio's Daring Journey.

Meet Mickey Mouse features renowned characters such as Mickey Mouse, Minnie Mouse, and Donald Duck.

Plaza Gardens Restaurant serves a superb lunch that combines typical Disney dishes with French delicacies.

Evening:
Witness the stunning evening parade, Disney
Illuminations, which includes bright floats, popular
characters, and a breathtaking fireworks finale.
Witness the exciting midnight change of Space
Mountain: Mission 2 into Hyperspace Mountain:
Rebellion.
Finish your wonderful day with a character dining
experience at Auberge Cendrillon, Cinderella's
lovely castle restaurant.

Itinerary 2: Family Fun Adventure (2 Days)
This route is intended for families with small
children and features a slow pace with lots of stops
and character interactions.

Day 1:
Arrive mid-morning and proceed to Fantasyland,
where children may go on a swashbuckling
adventure with Peter Pan and soar over the sky with
Dumbo.
Plaza Inn Restaurant offers a character dining
experience, including a delicious breakfast or lunch
with favorite Disney characters.

Discover Toon Studio, home to the zany world of Roger Rabbit and the thrilling ride Cars: Quatre Roues Rallye.

Enjoy a peaceful sail along the Rivers of the World in Adventureland, followed by a meet-and-greet with characters such as Pocahontas and Baloo.

In the afternoon, visit Frontierland for a thrilling ride on the Big Thunder Mountain Railroad and a tour of Phantom Manor.

Finish the day with the nighttime extravaganza, Disney Illuminations.

Day 2:

Begin the day in Discoveryland, where families can go on a thrilling space voyage with Buzz Lightyear Laser Blast and discover the marvels of the ocean with Nemo's Submarine Voyage.

Cowboy Cookout Barbecue in Frontierland serves a character meal with a sense of the Wild West.

In the afternoon, visit Walt Disney Studios Park for a day full of cinematic magic. At the Animation Celebration, guests may ride The Twilight Zone Tower of Terror™ and learn about animation.

Finish your wonderful excursion with a character-eating experience at Disney Junior Play 'n Dine, which includes a meet-and-greet with your favorite Disney Junior characters.

Itinerary 3: Thrills and Chills for Adults (2-3 Days)

This schedule is designed for thrill-seekers and people seeking a more immersed experience beyond the coasters. Prepare for lengthier wait times at popular attractions.

Day 1:

Arrive early and head straight for thrilling coasters like Hyperspace Mountain: Mission 2 and Indiana Jones and the Temple of Peril.

Explore Adventureland, including the spectacular Indiana Jones and the Temple of Peril and Pirates of the Caribbean.

Enjoy a delicious meal at Agrabah Cafe, which features cuisine from Disney's Aladdin.

In the afternoon, explore Discoveryland, taking on the high-speed thrills of Hyperspace Mountain:

journey 2 and embark on a daring space journey on Buzz Lightyear Laser Blast.
Witness Disney Illuminations, a fascinating twilight extravaganza.

Day 2:
Walt Disney Studios Park offers a variety of theatrical events and parades. With Disney Junior Live on Stage, you may immerse yourself in the world of its characters! Come be enchanted by Disney's beautiful twilight spectacle, Stars on Parade. Finish your day with a behind-the-scenes peek at cinematic magic on the Studio Tram Tour: Behind the Magic!

Explore Hidden Gems: Go beyond the thrill rides to uncover Disneyland Park's hidden gems. Take a terrifying voyage through Phantom Manor, a ghostly house filled with mystery. Take a delightful adventure through Alice's Curious Labyrinth, a maze inspired by Alice in Wonderland. Catch a live performance of The Lion King: Rhythm of the Pride Lands, a spectacular musical tribute to the legendary Disney film.

Indulge in Fine Dining: Enjoy a luxury dining experience at one of Disneyland's premier restaurants. Monsieur Paul, located on Main Street, USA, serves French gourmet food. Bella Notte invites you on a gastronomic adventure through Italy, complete with a beautiful atmosphere and wonderful Italian gastronomy.

Disneyland Park changes after dark, offering exciting nocturnal activities. Witness the spectacular fireworks show, Disney Illuminations, and the exciting nighttime transition of Space Mountain: Mission 2 into Hyperspace Mountain: Rebellion. Attend a late-night performance of one of the park's several stage productions, such as Mickey's PhilharMagic or The Lion King: Rhythm of the Pride Lands.

Day 3:
Explore Paris: Spend a day visiting the colorful city of Paris. Visit famous monuments such as the Eiffel Tower and the Louvre Museum, or stroll

down the Champs-Élysées. Discover Paris' rich culture and history at your leisure.

Relax and Recharge: Take a break from the park and spend some time at your hotel. Relax by the pool, have a spa treatment, or visit the shops and restaurants surrounding Disneyland Paris.

Spend a whole day touring Walt Disney Studios Park. The Twilight Zone Tower of Terror™ and Rock 'n' Roller Coaster Starring Aerosmith provide thrilling rides.
Marvel Studios' Character Academy immerses you in the realm of superheroes, where you may meet legendary characters such as Iron Man and Captain America.

Remember, these are only beginning points to help you plan your Disneyland Paris vacation. Personalize your schedule according to your interests, preferred pace, and length of stay. With careful planning and this guide by your side, you're guaranteed to enjoy a spectacular and unforgettable time at Disneyland Paris in 2024!

Enchanted Efficiency: Disneyland Paris'

Transportation System: Trains, Buses, and More! Ahoy, mates! Welcome back to the enchanted shores of Disneyland Paris! Now that you've seen the beauties of Paris outside the parks, let's take a closer look at the resort's efficient and charming transit system. Forget heavy compasses and confusing maps; Disneyland Paris provides easy navigation, so you can spend more time conquering exhilarating rides and seeing cherished characters. Batten down the hatches and get ready for a quick tour of the resort's transportation choices!

All Aboard the Magic Express:

For a completely seamless experience, consider using the official Disneyland Paris Express shuttle service. These luxury coaches will carry you directly from the airport (CDG or ORLY) to your Disney hotel, eliminating the need to navigate public transit or taxis upon arrival. Consider sitting back and relaxing after your journey, knowing that you'll be whisked away to the center of the fun in no time.

A Train Adventure: Marne-la-Vallée Chessy Station

Marne-la-Vallée Chessy station, located just a stone's throw away from the parks, serves as the entryway to Disneyland Paris for tourists coming by train. The efficient TGV high-speed train network connects major cities in France and Europe to this station, providing a quick and environmentally responsible option to get to the resort. After arriving at the station, a short walk or a brief ride on the free Marne-la-Vallée Chessy Loop train will take you immediately to the park gate.

Buses and Shuttles Connect Hotels and Parks
A network of free Disney Buses runs throughout
the resort, providing easy transportation between
all Disney Hotels, Disney Village, Disneyland Park,
and Walt Disney Studios Park. These roomy and
pleasant buses operate often, resulting in short wait
times.

Horseless Carriages and Trains:
Embrace Disneyland Paris' vintage appeal with the
Main Street Vehicles. Board a classic horse-drawn
trolley or omnibus and take a leisurely journey
down Main Street, U.S.A., adding a bit of fairytale
romance to your park experience.

Disneyland Railroad: A Scenic Journey
Embark on a colorful trip on the Disneyland
Railroad, a beautiful train that circuits both
Disneyland and Walt Disney Studios parks. This
classic attraction provides a beautiful tour around
the parks, allowing you to see hidden features and
monuments from a different angle. It's an excellent
opportunity to relax your tired legs while taking in
the wonderful surroundings.

Shanks' Mare (Walking): Never underestimate the strength of your own two feet! Disneyland Paris is meant to be a pedestrian-friendly destination, with lovely paths and themed sections that invite exploring. Walking allows you to find hidden nuances, capture beautiful images, and fully immerse yourself in the beauty at your speed.

A Mobile Application for Smooth Sailing: Before you visit Disneyland Paris, download the official app. This useful application provides real-time wait times for attractions, thorough park maps that emphasize transit alternatives, and even the ability to mobile order meals, assuring a seamless and efficient park visit.

A final word on enchantment: Disneyland Paris' transportation system is created with guests' convenience in mind. Whether you take a high-speed rail, a fanciful train trip, or a stroll, exploring the resort is simple. Relax, enjoy the ride, and be ready to be carried away by the enchantment that greets you at every turn!

Disneyland Park: A Journey Through Timeless Stories

Hello, explorers of all ages! Today, we begin on an enthralling journey across Disneyland Park, the crown gem of Disneyland Paris. Located in 48°52′26″N 2°31′52″E, this magical world connects us to cherished stories and iconic characters, promising an unforgettable trip packed with laughter, thrills, and a generous dose of pixie dust. So grab your map, fix your captain's hat, and prepare to go on a fantastic voyage through time!

Main Street, United States of America: Step Back in Time and Down Memory Lane on

Our journey begins at the heart of Disneyland Park, the lovely and nostalgic Main Street, U.S.A. Walking down this brick-lined boulevard is like stepping back in time to a turn-of-the-century American village. Victorian-era buildings with beautiful features flank the street, their flags fluttering in the soft air. Horseless carriages transporting families ride down the center, adding to the air of nostalgia. The scent of freshly made cookies and popcorn permeates the air, enticing you to indulge in classic pleasures.

As you travel down Main Street, USA, keep an eye out for these hidden beauties

Disneyland Railroad Station: Located at the end of Main Street, this majestic Victorian-style edifice serves as the departure point for a fanciful train journey throughout the park. Make sure to take a snapshot in front of the renowned locomotive for a lasting memory. (48°52'26"N 2°31'52"E)

Disney Clothiers, Ltd.: Fashionistas of all ages will be delighted by this delightful boutique brimming with Disney-inspired apparel and accessories. From Mickey Mouse ears to Cinderella-inspired outfits, there's something for everyone to add a little enchantment to their look. (48°52'26"N 2°31'52"E)

The Emporium is a huge department store filled with Disney products. The Emporium sells everything from plush toys to souvenirs, clothes, and home décor. Prepare to spend some time wandering the aisles and choosing the ideal souvenir for your vacation. (48°52'26"N 2°31'52"E)

Encounters with Favorite Characters:
Main Street, USA is also a popular spot for character meet-and-greets. Mickey Mouse, Minnie Mouse, Donald Duck, Daisy Duck, and their companions frequently come throughout the day, ready to shake hands, sign autographs, and pose for photographs. It's a heartwarming opportunity to make lifelong experiences, particularly for young travelers.

A Tapestry of Entertainment:
Don't miss out on the wonderful street entertainment as you go along Main Street. Energetic jazz bands play toe-tapping melodies, while energetic Disney characters like Goofy and Pluto engage with guests, creating a dynamic ambiance that sets the tone for a magical day.

A Culinary Adventure Awaits:
Main Street, U.S.A. has a wonderful range of eating alternatives to suit all tastes. Enjoy a traditional American dinner at Plaza Inn, a scoop of ice cream at Disneyland Railroad Refreshments, or a warm cup of coffee and a croissant at Starbucks.

The Castle in Sight: Set Sail for Adventure Lands

As you approach the end of Main Street, U.S.A., a spectacular sight awaits Sleeping Beauty Castle. This towering monument, embellished with elaborate embellishments and dazzling spires, is Disneyland Park's unmistakable emblem. It's a magnificent reminder that fairy tales do come true, as well as a springboard to many more amazing experiences.

A Few Tips for Navigating Main Street, USA:
Take your time: Main Street, U.S.A. is a place to unwind, absorb the ambiance, and admire the subtle details. Do not rush through; instead, take photographs, visit the stores, and enjoy the street entertainment.

Be Aware of Crowds: Main Street, U.S.A. may become congested, particularly during high seasons. Be patient, maneuver nicely, and keep an eye on little children.

Download the Disneyland Paris app: The app includes wait times for attractions, show schedules, and character meet-and-greet places, helping you to arrange your day more effectively.

Main Street, United States of America is more than simply an entryway; it's the heart and spirit of Disneyland Park. It sets the tone for the day's adventures, promising awe, nostalgia, and timeless stories. Now with a full heart and a growling stomach.

Frontierland: Yee hoo! Lassoing Adventures in the Wild West

Saddle up, partners! Our amazing adventure through Disneyland Park continues as we head over to Frontierland, a fascinating area steeped in the spirit of the Wild West. This dusty outpost at the park's far end (pun intended!) takes you back in time to saloons, shootouts, and gold miners looking for a fortune. Hold on to your hats, because Frontierland offers an amazing trip full of rootin' tootin' excitement for the entire family.

The Enchanting Atmosphere of Frontierland
Frontierland transports you to a bygone age from the minute you enter. Towering timber structures with swinging saloon doors fill the sandy lanes. The music features lively rural songs and the occasional clip-clop of horses. Actors costumed in historical garb enhance the immersive experience by greeting guests with a pleasant "howdy" and instilling a feeling of authenticity. Keep a lookout for wandering cowboys, bank robbers (don't worry, they're nice!) and the occasional Can-Can dancer kicking up her heels.

Thrilling Expeditions Await
Frontierland has a variety of thrilling rides that will send thrills down your spine and leave you with a big smile. Here are a few highlights that cannot be missed:

Big Thunder Mountain Railroad: Set off on a runaway mine train adventure through a dangerous gold mine. This exhilarating roller coaster offers startling dips, steep bends, and stunning vistas of the park. Hold hold tight for a crazy journey! (The minimum height requirement is 102 cm or 3 ft 4 in.)

Thunder Mesa Riverboat Landing: Set sail on the Far West's rivers on an authentic paddle steamer. This peaceful excursion takes you on a picturesque tour around Frontierland, revealing hidden elements and giving a pleasant breather from the faster-paced activities. (The minimum height requirement is any height.)

Sharpshooting Skills and Frontier Fun

Want to put your sharpshooting talents to the test? Go to the Rustler Roundup Shootin' Gallery to shoot animated targets and get points. This traditional carnival-style game is entertaining for the entire family, including the youngest cowboys and cowgirls. (An additional cost applies.)

For the Young Buckaroos

Frontierland welcomes explorers of all ages. Little ones will love Pocahontas' Indian Village, a delightful play area where they can climb teepees, navigate a totem pole maze, and even meet Pocahontas herself! (The minimum height requirement is any height.)

Fueling Up for Adventure

After a hectic trip across the Wild West, you're sure to work up an appetite. Frontierland has a wide range of food alternatives to satiate your cravings:

Colonel Hathi's Pizza Outpost: Start your next excursion with a delicious slice of pizza from this rustic café.

Cowboy Cookout Barbecue: Enjoy meaty barbecue dishes including ribs, chicken, and baked beans served picnic-style in a gorgeous outdoor environment.

Last Chance Saloon: For a taste of the Wild West, stop by this vibrant salon and quench your thirst with a cool beverage (alcoholic and non-alcoholic alternatives available).

Some Tips for Conquering Frontierland:
Consider utilizing FastPass+ to avoid excessive wait times at Big Thunder Mountain Railroad, which is a popular ride.

Shady Retreats: Frontierland may be rather sunny, especially during the summer. If you need to chill off, go to an air-conditioned business or restaurant.

Showtimes: Check the show calendar for performances by the Frontierland Players, a brilliant group of performers that bring the Wild West to life via music and dance.

Frontierland is a place of adventure, excitement, and a hint of nostalgia. So, throw on your spurs, grab your hat, and prepare to lasso some amazing moments in this exhilarating Wild West! Our tour around Disneyland Park continues with a thrilling experience in Adventureland. Stay tuned, partners!

Adventureland: Uncovering Hidden Treasures and Exotic Thrills

Ahoy, mates! Buckle your swashbuckling belts and prepare to sail for strange beaches! Our enchanting journey around Disneyland Paris continues as we enter Adventureland, a region filled with hidden riches, adventurous excursions, and intriguing encounters. This enthralling realm, nestled at the base of Sleeping Beauty Castle, takes you to a world of pirates, rainforests, and ancient civilizations, guaranteeing an exciting trip for explorers of any age.

A Breathtaking Arrival

Entering Adventureland is like passing through a time warp. Towering waterfalls stream over thick greenery, providing a pleasant and immersive environment. The air is filled with strange bird songs and the rhythmic chanting of invisible people. Wooden structures reminiscent of colonial ports flank the twisting passageways, their aged exterior hinting at the thrills that await inside. Keep a watch out for roving explorers, naughty monkeys swinging through the treetops, and the occasional pirate scheming their next treasure robbery.

Exciting Expeditions for the Adventurous Soul
Adventureland has a variety of thrilling attractions that will send thrills down your spine and fire your spirit of adventure. Here are a few highlights that will have you wanting more:

Pirates of the Caribbean: Take a daring boat journey through the lawless town of Maracaibo and the perilous waterways of the Caribbean. Navigate caverns, combat phantom pirates, and enjoy exhilarating drops and amazing effects with Captain Jack Sparrow and a memorable ensemble of characters. (The minimum height requirement is 102 cm or 3 ft 4 in.)

Indiana Jones and the Temple of Peril: Hold on to your hats as you speed through a collapsing temple in a runaway mining car adventure. This high-speed coaster has startling drops, abrupt curves, and thrilling spectacular effects that will make you gasp. (The minimum height requirement is 102 cm or 3 ft 4 in.)

Exploring Uncharted Territory

Adventureland offers more than simply thrilling thrills. It's a world packed with immersive activities that will make you feel like a genuine adventurer. Here are a few adventures you shouldn't miss:

Swiss Family Robinson Treehouse: Climb shaky ladders to discover the Robinson family's elaborately designed treehouse. Discover hidden rooms, take in the panoramic vistas, and be transported into the realm of this timeless story. (The minimum height requirement is any height.)

La Fontaine des Elephants (The Elephant Fountain): Relax at this lovely fountain with joyful elephants spouting water. It's an ideal area to unwind, cool down, and take some great shots. Tantalising Treats for Explorers

After a day of exhilarating activities and unusual discoveries, you're sure to build up an appetite. Adventureland has a range of food alternatives that will excite your taste buds:

Adventureland Restaurant: Take a gourmet trip across the South Pacific with a cuisine influenced by Polynesian and Asian tastes.

Captain Hook's Galley: This pirate-themed restaurant serves you a delicious burger and a basket of golden fries.

The Tropical Club: Refresh yourself with a Dole Whip, a pineapple and soft-serve ice cream dessert that has become a Disneyland Paris classic.

A Few Tips for Conquering Adventure Land:
FastPass+ Consideration: Pirates of the Caribbean and Indiana Jones and the Temple of Peril are both popular attractions, so consider purchasing Disney Premier Access or utilizing a FastPass+ to avoid excessive lines.

Rider Switch Option: If you're traveling with small children who don't fit the height requirements for several attractions, use the Rider Switch feature. This permits one parent to wait with the youngster while the other enjoys the ride, after which they can trade places.

Showtimes: Check the show schedule for Adventureland's entertainers. Through music, dance, and acrobatics, these gifted performers bring the worlds of pirates, rainforests, and ancient civilizations alive.

Adventureland is a place that inspires the imagination and wakes the explorer inside. So take your compass, put on your pith helmet, and prepare to discover hidden treasures and enjoy exotic thrills in this enthralling environment! Our tour around Disneyland Park continues with a wonderful getaway to Fantasyland. Batten down the hatches, mateys, and prepare for another adventure!

Fantasyland: Soaring Through Fairytales and Meeting Favorite Characters

Hello, visionaries and believers of all ages! Our fanciful journey around Disneyland Paris takes a surreal turn when we visit Fantasyland, a world where beloved stories come to life and childhood dreams come true. Fantasyland, located beneath the watchful eyes of Sleeping Beauty Castle, is a brilliant tapestry of colorful landscapes, beautiful music, and beloved characters that await you around every turn. So, release your inner kid, sprinkle some pixie dust, and get ready to soar through a world of classic fairytales!

A Fairytale Awaits

Walking inside Fantasyland is like entering the pages of a favorite fairytale. The air is magically shimmering, and the brilliant colors and fanciful buildings take you to a realm of pure fantasy. Lush vegetation, flowing waterfalls, and beautiful cottages make for a magical environment that will take your breath away. Melodies from iconic Disney flicks flood the air, heightening the lovely mood and setting the stage for extraordinary interactions. Keep a lookout for cheerful fairies fluttering through the flowers, cheeky chipmunks scampering across walkways, and the rare glimpse of a princess walking through the park.

Encounters With Fairytale Royalty
Fantasyland provides a unique opportunity to meet some of your favorite Disney characters in person. Imagine the delight on a child's face as they embrace Mickey Mouse, sip tea with Cinderella, or giggle with Goofy! Character meet-and-greet spots are distributed over the nation, with wait durations varying based on the character's popularity. Download the Disneyland Paris app to check character availability and plan your encounters for a truly spectacular experience.

Exciting Adventures for Every Dreamer
Fantasyland is more than simply meet & greets and fantastical surroundings. It also has thrilling attractions that will send shivers down your spine and make you desire more. Here are a few gems that will stir your imagination:

Peter Pan's Flight: Fly through the skies above Neverland on a fanciful adventure with Peter Pan and his buddies. This suspended dark ride transports you through key sequences from the renowned film, providing a lovely escape into the realm of childlike wonder. (The minimum height requirement is 102 cm or 3 ft 4 in.)

Le Passage Enchanté d'Aladdin (The Enchanted Passage of Aladdin): Aladdin, Jasmine, and Genie take a magical carpet trip across Agrabah. This magical tour experience includes breathtaking animations, compelling music, and spectacular effects that bring the world of Aladdin to life. (The minimum height requirement is any height.)

Classic Adventures for All Ages
Fantasyland has a range of attractions for adventurers of all ages. Here are some timeless gems you shouldn't miss:
Pinocchio's Daring Journey: Climb on a fanciful boat and negotiate Monstro the whale's tortuous canals in this delightful dark ride. Discover

legendary moments from the Pinocchio narrative and feel the thrill of a surprise drop. (The minimum height requirement is any height.)

Mad Hatter's Tea Cups: This famous Fantasyland attraction offers a fanciful spin in a huge teacup. The brilliant colors, lively music, and dizzying twirls will put a grin on your face. (The minimum height requirement is any height.)

A feast fit for a fairytale.

After a whirlwind journey through magical forests, soaring sky, and storybook castles, you're sure to be hungry. Fantasyland has a wide range of food alternatives to satiate your cravings:

L'Auberge de Cendrillon (Cinderella's Inn): This charming restaurant will make your dreams of dining in a fairytale castle come true. Indulge in a great lunch inspired by French cuisine while surrounded by Disney enchantment. (Reservations are highly advised).

Le Petit Coin des Gourmandises de Blanche Neige (Snow White's Hungry Bear Restaurant) is a quick-service restaurant that serves typical foods like burgers, fries, and salads. It is ideal for a relaxed lunch or supper.

Fantasyland Village Treats: For a fast snack or a refreshing treat, try a Mickey Mouse-shaped ice cream bar, a crispy churro, or a fruit cup.

Tips for Enhancing Your Fantasyland Experience:

FastPass+ Consideration: Popular attractions such as Peter Pan's Flight might have lengthy wait periods. Consider purchasing Disney Premier Access or using FastPass+ to make the most of your time at Fantasyland.

Plan for Crowds: Fantasyland is a popular destination, particularly during peak seasons. Prepare for crowds and use common courtesy, especially if you have young children.

Interactive aspects: Many attractions in Fantasyland include interactive aspects. Keep an eye out for hidden Mickey.

Discoveryland: Warp Speed into the Future and Beyond the Stars

Hello, space cadets and intrepid adventurers! Our rapid tour of Disneyland Paris takes a futuristic turn as we blast off into Discoveryland. This domain of invention and cosmic travel brings you to a world of shimmering chrome, fascinating contraptions, and mind-bending experiences. So saddle in, calibrate your jetpacks, and get ready to blast into the future and beyond the stars!

A Shining Vision of Tomorrow

Stepping into Discoveryland is like stepping upon a page from a science fiction story. Sleek, futuristic towers made of glass and steel pierce the sky, their dazzling surfaces reflecting the colorful lights and enticing sounds of this wonderful world. Towering rocket ships stand ready to launch, while odd, alien spacecraft hum with hidden power. The soundtrack is a frenetic mix of electronic music and futuristic sound effects that immediately transports you to a universe where everything is possible. Keep a watch out for roving robots, excited scientists, and the occasional cast member costumed as a futuristic spacefarer.

Exciting Adventures for the Modern Explorer
Discoveryland offers a variety of thrilling activities that will propel you through time and space. Here are a few highlights that are sure to spark your spirit of adventure:

Hyperspace Mountain Mission 2: Prepare to take off on an amazing space journey aboard a high-speed coaster. This thrilling journey includes explosive drops, unexpected turns, and stunning special effects that will make you feel as if you've been to another galaxy. (The minimum height requirement is 132 cm or 4 feet 4 inches.)

Buzz Lightyear Laser Blast: Join Buzz Lightyear on his adventure to battle the evil Emperor Zurg! Embark in a cosmic adventure through dynamic play zones, using your laser blaster to zap targets and earn points. This attraction is popular with space rangers of all ages. (The minimum height requirement is any height.)

Discovering the Mysteries of the Cosmos
Discoveryland is about more than simply
heart-pounding thrills. It's also a place that inspires
curiosity and wonder about the cosmos. Here are
some experiences that will take you on an exciting
voyage of discovery:

Orbitron: Soar through the skies in a quirky flying
vehicle that provides amazing views of Disneyland
Park. This iconic attraction is the ideal way to
unwind while seeing Discoveryland's futuristic
surroundings. (The minimum height requirement
is any height.)
**Les Mystères du Nautilus (The Mysteries of the
Nautilus):** Journey to the depths of the ocean
aboard Captain Nemo's famed submarine, the
Nautilus. This walkthrough experience includes
breathtaking underwater scenery, intriguing
animatronics, and a view into the mysteries of the
deep sea. (The minimum height requirement is any
height.)

Fueling up for your Intergalactic Adventure
After a dizzying journey across time and space,
you're sure to have a cosmic hunger. Discoveryland
has several eating alternatives to satiate your
appetites for futuristic cuisine:

Eatery Agrabah Café: Take a gourmet trip
through the realm of Aladdin at this delightful
eatery. Enjoy a variety of Middle Eastern-inspired
meals in a lively and colorful atmosphere.
Cosmic Restaurant: Prepare for your next
excursion with quick-service alternatives such as
burgers, fries, and pizza. The restaurant has a
futuristic space concept, replete with porthole
windows and glittering stars.
Grab a cool drink, a sweet snack, or a Mickey
Mouse-shaped ice cream bar from the Hyperion
Refreshment Station.

A Few Tips for Conquering Discoveryland:
FastPass+ Consideration: Popular rides, such as
Hyperspace Mountain Mission 2, might have
lengthy wait times. Consider purchasing Disney

Premier Access or using FastPass+ to make the most of your time in Discoveryland.

Height limitations: Certain Discoveryland attractions have height limitations. Check these limits before visiting a certain attraction to prevent disappointment.

Showtimes: Check the concert calendar for performances by Stitch Live! Animated show. This interactive experience, which features everyone's favorite troublemaking alien, is sure to make people of all ages grin.

Discoveryland is a region that stretches the bounds of imagination and inspires curiosity about the future. So, put on your spacesuit, grab your jetpack, and be ready to explore the universe, conquer daring adventures, and see the wonder of tomorrow in this extraordinary place! Our voyage around Disneyland Park culminates with a stunning evening show on Main Street, U.S.A., which has retained its ageless beauty. Stay tuned, space adventurers, for the great conclusion!

Disneyland Park for All: Accessibility & Special Services

Disneyland Paris is devoted to providing a fantastic and inclusive experience for people of all abilities. This guide emphasizes the accessible features and unique services offered throughout the park, ensuring that everyone can experience the marvels of Disneyland Park.

Accessibility Features:
Park Accessibility Map: A printable park map shows accessible paths, toilets, attractions, and dedicated pick-up and drop-off areas for guests in wheelchairs and mobility scooters.
Wheelchair Rentals: Disneyland Paris provides manual and electric wheelchair rentals to customers who require them. These can be reserved ahead of time or on-site at the park.
Companion Care: Guests with impairments may be eligible for a companion care access pass. This pass lets a chosen companion help the traveler wait in lines, board attractions, and navigate the park.

Hearing loops are offered at many attractions and theaters to help people with hearing aids hear better.

Visual Cues: Some attractions use flashing lights or strobe effects. A list of these attractions is provided upon request to assist people with photosensitivity in making informed decisions.

Trained service animals are accepted in Disneyland Park. Disney even has specific pet rest facilities for increased convenience.

Special Services:

Disability Access Service (DAS): This service enables customers with cognitive difficulties to bypass regular queues. By registering with Guest Services, tourists obtain a return time to see the attraction, avoiding long wait periods that can be daunting for certain visitors.

Sensory Guides: These downloadable guides identify possible sensory triggers within certain sites and offer recommendations for guests with sensory sensitivities to navigate these locations.

Relaxation Areas: Calm rooms scattered around the park provide a tranquil haven for tourists seeking a respite from the rush and bustle.

Cast Member Assistance: Disneyland Paris Cast Members are easily accessible to help customers with impairments. They can provide you with directions, answer inquiries, and assist you explore the park's numerous attractions.

Plan Your Visit:

Pre-Arrival Planning: Review the Disneyland Paris website's Accessibility Guide. This thorough guide describes accessible attractions, services, and park characteristics.

Contact Guest Services: We are delighted to address any accessibility-related inquiries you may have before or during your stay. They may be reached over the phone or via the Disneyland Paris app.

Download the Disneyland Paris app, which includes wait times, performance schedules, and a park map with accessible items highlighted. Remember:

Disneyland Paris aspires to provide a fantastic experience for everybody. Guests of all abilities may experience Disneyland Park's delights and thrills by taking advantage of its accessible features and unique services. For further information or if you have any questions, please contact Disneyland Paris Guest Services. Now, with a heart full of fairy dust and memories to treasure, let's return to Main Street, USA, for a sparkling midnight extravaganza!

Walt Disney Studios Park: Lights, Camera, Action!

Welcome, moviegoers and animation enthusiasts! Buckle up for a thrilling behind-the-scenes experience at Walt Disney Studios Park, a land dedicated to cinematic magic and the beautiful world of animation. This park, located at 48°52′18″N 2°32′12″E, immerses visitors in the Golden Age of Hollywood, bringing great films and beloved characters to life. So, grab your popcorn, put on your director's hat, and be ready to be whisked away on an exciting voyage through the fascinating world of filmmaking!

Front Lot: Hollywood Glamour, Tinseltown Dreams

Our tour begins in the heart of Walt Disney Studios Park, on the intriguing Front Lot. Walking down this crowded road is like going back in time to the golden age of Hollywood. Towering Art Deco buildings with sparkling neon signage flank the boulevard, their façade depicting popular scenes and characters from Disney and Pixar films. Vintage automobiles travel in the middle lane, adding a nostalgic feel. The air is alive with the sounds of street performers, frenetic music, and eager talk, creating a vivid and immersive environment. Keep a look out for wandering Disney Junior characters such as Mickey Mouse and Minnie Mouse, who like greeting tourists and posing for photographs.

A Celebration of Disney and Pixar Films

The Front Lot is a visual feast for cinema fans, including nods to old and recent Disney and Pixar films. Here are some highlights you shouldn't miss:

The Hollywood Tower Hotel, inspired by the renowned Hollywood Tower Hotel from the

"Twilight Zone" television series, towers above the skyline. While not now working, it is a mesmerizing reminder of Disney's ability to combine imagination with Hollywood history. (48°52'18"N 2°32'12"E)

Animation Patio: This lovely patio celebrates the beauty of Disney and Pixar animation. Here, you'll find lovely stores filled with items depicting your favorite animated characters, interactive activities celebrating the animation process, and even the opportunity to meet some of your favorite Disney Junior performers!

Thrilling Performances and Captivating Entertainment

The Front Lot is more than simply eye-catching architecture and nostalgia. It's also a venue for thrilling performances and engaging entertainment. Here are a few experiences you should not miss:

Mickey's PhilharMagic: Immerse yourself in a fantastic musical journey through legendary Disney flicks with this magnificent 3D theater experience.

Laugh along with Donald Duck, marvel at the animation's genius, and let the music take you to your favorite Disney places. (The minimum height requirement is any height.)

Disney Junior Live On Stage! This interactive stage event allows you to sing and dance alongside your favorite Disney Junior characters. This presentation is ideal for young travelers, with live music, fun costumes, and amazing experiences with beloved characters. (Showtimes change; see the Disneyland Paris app for information.)

A Culinary Adventure Awaits
After such a fast-paced introduction to the world of movies, you're sure to get hungry. The Front Lot has a wide range of food alternatives to satiate your cravings:

Studio 1 Restaurant: Take a gourmet tour around the world with this elegant restaurant. The menu includes meals influenced by world cuisine, providing a tasty retreat for discriminating palates. (Reservations are advised.)

Disney Junior Dining: This delightful restaurant allows young travelers to dine with their favorite Disney Junior characters. The colorful and cheerful atmosphere serves typical children's meals, making it an ideal destination for families with young children.

Here are some Tips for Conquering the Front lot:
Download the Disneyland Paris App: The app displays wait times for performances, character meet-and-greet places, and restaurant availability, helping you to arrange your day more effectively.

Showtimes: Check the show schedule for Mickey's PhilharMagic and Disney Junior Live on Stage! make sure you don't miss out on these exciting activities.

Keep a look out for interactive features in the Front Lot. You can come upon hidden Mickeys or amusing surprises that enhance the immersive experience.

The Front Lot serves as a colorful entry point into Walt Disney Studios Park's immersive universe. It sets the tone for a day full of cinematic enchantment, animation marvels, and exhilarating experiences. So, with a heart full of joy and a camera full of memories, let us explore further into the enchanting world of film! Our next trip is to Toon Studio, a crazy and fascinating realm where favorite Disney cartoons come alive. Stay tuned, moviegoers, as the adventure continues!

Toon Studio: Joining Your Favorite Cartoon Characters for Zany Antics

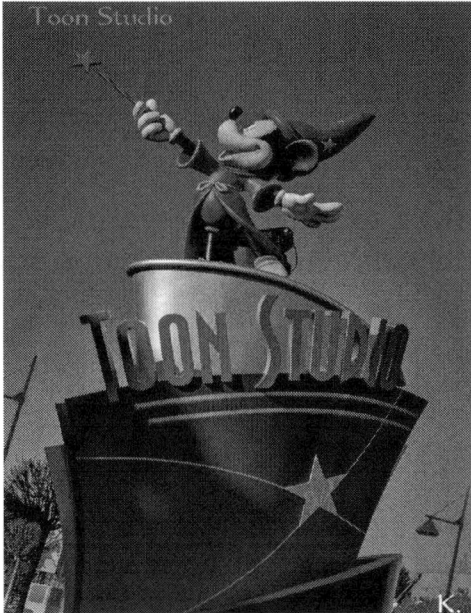

Welcome back, animation aficionados! Our fanciful journey through Walt Disney Studios Park continues as we enter Toon Studio, an area packed with crazy cartoon characters, great Disney flicks, and hilarious experiences. Toon Studio, located within the park, takes visitors to a world inspired by the golden age of animation, where everything is bigger than life, colors are impossibly vivid, and slapstick humor reigns supreme. So, loosen up your funny bone, grab a huge paintbrush (figuratively, of course!), and get ready to join your favorite cartoon characters for a day of hilarious fun!

A Celebration of Classic Animation

Walking into Toon Studio is like entering the pages of a favorite comic book. Buildings resemble enormous cartoon props, with brightly colored façade and exaggerated features. Quirky sound effects and amusing music flood the air, creating a charmingly chaotic atmosphere. Keep a watch out for cheeky chipmunks scampering over roofs, lively ducks wreaking havoc, and the odd glimpse of a towering Disney villain lurking in the shadows (just joking... kinda).

Exciting Rides and Cartoon Chaos

Toon Studio has a variety of exciting attractions that will have you laughing, shouting, and wishing for more cartoon mayhem. Here are a few highlights that will tickle your funny bone:

The Twilight Zone Tower of Terror™ is a spectacular freefall experience at the Hollywood Tower Hotel that will have you screaming. Take a thrilling adventure through the hotel's dark hallways, experiencing surprising drops and unsettling visual effects inspired by the classic "Twilight Zone" television show. (The minimum height requirement is 102 cm or 3 ft 4 in.)

Cars Route 66 Road Trip: Join Lightning McQueen and Mater on a wild adventure through Radiator Springs! This family-friendly coaster has surprising turns, amusing surprises, and breathtaking recreations of memorable sequences from the popular "Cars" film franchise. (The minimum height requirement is 102 cm or 3 ft 4 in.)

Interactive Experiences and Character Encounters

Toon Studio offers more than simply exhilarating rides. It's also a realm full of interactive activities and character interactions that bring your favorite cartoons to life. Here are several ways to join in on the animated fun:

Animation Academy: Unleash your inner animator and discover the secrets of Disney's renowned animation methods. This interactive game allows you to build your short animation sequence, bringing you on an intriguing trip through the realm of cartoon production. (The minimum height requirement is any height.)

Meet and Greet with Beloved Characters: Have you ever wanted to embrace Roger Rabbit or shake hands with Mickey Mouse? Toon Studio gives you the opportunity to meet some of your favorite Disney characters in person. Character meet-and-greet spots are distributed over the nation, with wait durations varying based on the character's popularity.

Fueling Up for Cartoon Chaos

After a rapid tour of the wild world of cartoons, you'll undoubtedly have a ravenous hunger. Toon Studio has a wide range of eating alternatives to satiate your demands for cartoon-themed treats:

Restaurant en Coulisses (Backstage Restaurant): At this delightful restaurant, you may go behind the scenes and experience the world of animation. The menu offers traditional French cuisine with a whimsical twist, delivered in an environment evocative of a cartoon animator's workshop. (Reservations are advised.)

Toon Studio Restaurant: This quick-service restaurant serves classics such as burgers, fries, and pizzas, making it ideal for a casual lunch or dinner. The lively and colorful environment will put a grin on your face.

A Few Tips for Conquering Toon Studios:

Consider using FastPass+ for popular attractions such as The Twilight Zone Tower of Terror™, which can have high wait times. To get the most out of your visit to Toon Studio, consider purchasing Disney Premier Access or using FastPass+. Height limitations: Some Toon Studio attractions have height limitations. Check these limits before visiting a certain attraction to prevent disappointment.

Keep a look out for interactive items in Toon Studio. You can come upon hidden Mickeys or amusing surprises that enhance the immersive experience.
Toon Studio is a world filled with fun, crazy characters, and vintage animation. So prepare to release your inner cartoon character, embrace the wackiness, and make amazing memories in this realm of pure, unadulterated fun! Our next visit takes us on an exciting journey through a galaxy far, far away in the heart of the Worlds of Pixar. Stay tuned, animation fans, as the adventure continues!

Worlds of Pixar: Immerse yourself in the vibrant worlds of Pixar animation

Welcome, Pixar fans! Prepare for a thrilling journey through Worlds of Pixar, a place dedicated to the inventive stories and compelling characters that have become synonymous with Pixar Animation Studios. Nestled within Walt Disney Studios Park, this vivid region transports you into the heart of your favorite Pixar films, allowing you to witness classic moments, meet beloved characters, and embark on thrilling adventures. So put on your thinking cap, adjust your Buzz Lightyear utility belt (figuratively, of course!), and get ready to get carried away on a tour through Pixar's endless inventiveness!

Kaleidoscope of Color and Imagination

Stepping into Worlds of Pixar is like entering a live, breathing Pixar film. Buildings replicate classic locales from favorite films, with colorful façade and quirky embellishments. Playful music from Pixar soundtracks permeates the air, immediately transporting you to familiar places. Larger-than-life character statues dot the landscape, providing ideal photo opportunities. Keep a watch out for roving Pixar companions including Woody, Jessie, and Miguel from Coco, who like greeting guests and sharing hugs (with agreement, of course!).

Exciting Adventures for Explorers of All Ages
Worlds of Pixar offers a variety of thrilling rides that will take you flying through the skies, careening through Radiator Springs, and plunging deep into the seas. Here are a few highlights that are sure to spark your spirit of adventure:

Hold on tight as you shrink down to the size of a toy vehicle and race through a massive Andy's room playset on this exhilarating family coaster. This fast-paced journey includes surprising drops, playful surprises, and a soundtrack of legendary "Toy Story" music. (The minimum height requirement is 102 cm or 3 ft 4 in.)
Cars Route 66 Road Trip: This exhilarating family coaster, also located in Toon Studio, provides an alternate experience within the World of Pixar. Buckle up for a wild ride around Radiator Springs with Lightning McQueen and Mater, complete

with surprising turns, fun surprises, and breathtaking recreations of classic sequences from the renowned "Cars" movie franchise. (The minimum height requirement is 102 cm or 3 ft 4 in.)

Interactive Experiences and Character Encounters
Worlds of Pixar is about more than simply heart-pounding thrills. It's also a realm full of interactive activities and character interactions that bring your favorite Pixar characters to life. Here are a few methods to get further into the world of Pixar:

Let your imagination run wild in this interactive play area inspired by "Toy Story." Climb atop enormous toys, explore creative buildings, and even meet some of your favorite characters from the film series. This is an ideal location for young adventurers to burn off energy and express their creativity. (The minimum height requirement is any height.)

Meet & Greets with Favorite Characters: Ever wanted to give Buzz Lightyear a high five or share a joke with Mike Wazowski? Worlds of Pixar gives you an opportunity to meet some of your favorite Pixar characters in person. Character meet-and-greet spots are distributed over the nation, with wait durations varying based on the character's popularity.

A Culinary Journey through Pixar Worlds
After a fast-paced journey through Pixar's bright worlds, you're sure to have a ravenous hunger. Worlds of Pixar has several eating alternatives to fulfill your appetite for Pixar-themed treats:

Pix'l Pizza Planet: Get ready for your next adventure with a slice of pizza or a refreshing drink at this restaurant inspired by Andy's favorite pizza parlor from "Toy Story." The vibrant and colorful setting will put a smile on your face, and the delicious menu items are ideal for a quick bite.
Remy's Ratatouille Kitchen: Shrink down to the size of a rat and embark on a gastronomic journey at this lovely restaurant inspired by the critically

acclaimed film "Ratatouille." The menu comprises excellent French cuisine, providing a wonderful fine dining experience in a playful atmosphere. (Reservations are highly advised).

A Few Tips for Conquering the World of Pixar:

FastPass+ Considerations: Popular attractions, such as RC Racer, might have significant wait times. Consider purchasing Disney Premier Access or using FastPass+ to make the most of your time at Worlds of Pixar.

Height Limits: Some Worlds of Pixar attractions have height limits. Check these limits before visiting a certain attraction to prevent disappointment.

Showtimes: Check the show schedule to see when the Pixar Pals Playtime will perform. This interactive stage play combines popular Pixar characters singing, dancing, and engaging with the audience, making it an ideal pastime for young explorers.

Marvel Avengers Campus: Joining Earth's Mightiest Heroes

Calling all superhero recruits! Buckle up and prepare to warp into the fascinating world of Marvel Avengers Campus, which is dedicated to the iconic Avengers and their remarkable allies. This immersive region at Disney California Adventure Park brings you to the middle of the action, where you can train alongside renowned heroes, face naughty villains, and feel the excitement of becoming a part of the ever-expanding Marvel Universe. So, gear up, unleash your inner hero, and get ready to assemble!

A Stark Industries Showcase

Stepping into Avengers Campus feels like entering the grounds of a cutting-edge Stark Industries facility. Towering industrial structures with the distinctive Avengers "A" insignia dominate the skyline. Futuristic vehicles, including Iron Man's famed repulsor ray-powered armor, are on show, with sleek shapes hinting at the incredible technology inside. The air is alive with activity, accented by the sounds of training drills, heroic proclamations, and the occasional humorous conversation amongst your favorite superheroes. Keep a look out for roving superheroes such as Black Widow, Captain America, and even the mischievous Loki lurking in the shadows (just joking... mainly).

Training for the Next Generation of Superheroes

Avengers Campus offers more than simply meet-and-greets and exhilarating thrills. It is a country committed to helping each guest reach their full potential. Here are a few ways you may train with the Avengers and find your inner hero:

WEB Slingers: A Spider-Man Adventure: Join Spider-Man on a quest to catch naughty Spider-Bots causing havoc around the Worldwide Engineering Brigade (WEB) headquarters. This novel, interactive experience uses augmented reality technology to let you sling webs alongside everyone's favorite web-slinger! (The minimum height requirement is any height.)

Guardians of the Galaxy - Mission: Breakout! Embark on an exciting voyage onboard the Milano, the Guardians of the Galaxy's quirky spacecraft. Help Rocket and his cheeky pals, Groot and Drax, escape The Collector's clutches on this thrilling reverse freefall coaster. (The minimum height requirement is 40 inches or 102 cm.)

Encountering Earth's Mighty Heroes

One of the attractions of Avengers Campus is the opportunity to meet your favorite superheroes. There are several methods to engage with these famous figures:

Heroic Encounters: Throughout the day, superheroes such as Captain America, Black Panther, and Iron Man may be seen walking the grounds, eager to welcome visitors, pose for photographs, and tell stories about their heroic deeds. Don't pass up this opportunity to make lasting moments with your favorite characters!

Character Dining: Share a wonderful lunch with some of your favorite superheroes at one of the many character dining experiences available across Avengers Campus. Share tales, take beautiful images, and make unforgettable memories with these renowned personalities. (Reservations are highly advised).

Fueling for Heroic Deeds

After a frenetic experience combating villains and training alongside the Avengers, you'll have a ravenous hunger. Avengers Campus has a wide range of food alternatives to satiate your demands for heroic fare:

Pym's Test Kitchen: Go on a gastronomic expedition where the servings are anything from average! Inspired by Hank Pym's remarkable shrinking and expanding technologies, this revolutionary eatery serves cuisine in supersized or microscopic amounts. Make sure to taste the famous Pym-ini Burger, which is a towering masterpiece that will satisfy even the most hungry hero!

Shawarma Palace: This restaurant, inspired by Tony Stark's favorite post-battle meal, serves exquisite shawarma wraps and falafel bowls. The rich cuisine and relaxed environment make this the ideal place to recharge before your next epic journey.

A Few Tips for Conquering the Avengers Campus:

Download the Disneyland App: The app displays wait times for attractions, character meet-and-greet places, and eating options, letting you organize your day more effectively.

Showtimes: Check the show calendar for unique performances and character encounters on Avengers Campus. Don't miss the spectacular feats and courageous performances!

Virtual line System: Some popular attractions on Avengers Campus use a virtual line system. To minimize excessive wait times, reserve your seat in line early using the Disneyland App.

Avengers Campus is a world that captivates your imagination and allows you to feel the excitement of becoming a superhero. So, unleash your inner hero, train with the Avengers, and make amazing moments in this country of the exceptional. Who knows, you could find out that you can be one of Earth's Mightiest Heroes after all!

Walt Disney Studios Park: A World of Magic Open to Everyone

The Walt Disney Studios Park seeks to provide an inclusive and memorable experience for guests of all abilities. This guide focuses on the accessible features and special services offered throughout the park, ensuring that everyone can experience the exhilarating rides, fascinating shows, and immersive environments.

Accessibility Features:

Park Accessibility Map: A printable park map shows accessible paths, toilets, attractions, and dedicated pick-up and drop-off areas for guests in wheelchairs and mobility scooters. The map also provides accessibility markers to help users find features such as captioned programs, assistive listening devices, and audio explanations.

Wheelchair Rentals: Disneyland Paris provides manual and electric wheelchair rentals to customers who require them. These can be reserved ahead of time or on-site at the park.

Companion Care: Guests with impairments may be eligible for a companion care access pass. This pass lets a chosen companion help the traveler wait in lines, board attractions, and navigate the park. Hearing loops are offered at many attractions and theaters to help people with hearing aids hear better.

Visual cues: Some attractions use flashing lights or strobe effects. A list of these attractions is provided upon request to assist people with photosensitivity in making informed decisions.

Trained service animals are accepted at Walt Disney Studios Park. Disney even has specific pet rest facilities for increased convenience.

Special Services:

Disability Access Service (DAS): This service enables customers with cognitive difficulties to bypass regular queues. By registering with Guest Services, tourists obtain a return time to see the attraction, avoiding long wait periods that can be daunting for certain visitors.

Sensory Guides: These downloadable guides identify possible sensory triggers within certain sites and offer recommendations for guests with sensory sensitivities to navigate these locations.

Relaxation Areas: Calm rooms positioned around the park provide a peaceful spot for customers who need to get away from the park's busy environment.
Cast Member Assistance: Disneyland Paris Cast Members are easily accessible to help customers with impairments. They can provide you with directions, answer inquiries, and assist you explore the park's numerous attractions.

Plan Your Visit:
Pre-Arrival Planning: Review the Disneyland Paris website's Accessibility Guide. This thorough guide describes accessible attractions, services, and park characteristics. Contact Guest Services before or during your visit if you have any accessibility-related queries, which they may address over the phone or via the Disneyland Paris app. Download the Disneyland Paris app, which includes wait times, performance schedules, and a park map with accessible items highlighted. This enables you to organize your day more effectively and locate accessible bathrooms, restaurants, and activities.

Remember:

Disneyland Paris is dedicated to providing a spectacular experience for everybody. Using the accessible features and unique services provided, guests of all abilities may experience the delights and thrills of Walt Disney Studios Park. For further information or if you have any questions, please contact Disneyland Paris Guest Services. Now, with a heart full of joy and an inclusive atmosphere, let's dig further into Disney Character Encounters.

Disney Character Encounters: Memories In The Making

One of the most magical features of a Disney Parks visit is getting to see your favorite Disney characters in person. These extraordinary interactions leave you with unforgettable memories, pure delight, and an unparalleled warm fuzzy sensation. Walt Disney Studios Park provides several opportunities to interact with iconic Disney heroes, princesses, villains (although not the genuinely wicked ones!), and whimsical buddies. So, grab out your signature book, put on your best grin, and prepare for a delightful experience in the realm of Disney character interactions!

Meet-and-Greet: A Face-to-Face Fairytale

Traditional meet-and-greets provide an invaluable chance for one-on-one engagement with Disney characters. These happy encounters are often held in specified areas across the park, with wait lengths ranging according to the character's popularity. Here's what to expect:

Character Greetings: Throughout Walt Disney Studios Park, there are dedicated spots where you may meet Mickey Mouse, Minnie Mouse, Donald Duck, and their companions. These locales are typically enhanced with bright backdrops that mirror the character's environment, resulting in an immersive experience. As you approach the designated location, a pleasant Cast Member will direct you through the queue to guarantee a seamless meet-and-greet.

Personalized Interactions: When it's your turn, greet your favorite character with a smile and wave! Cast Members excel at fostering these relationships, stimulating conversation, and creating a welcoming environment for customers of all ages. Feel free to request autographs, take photographs (flash photography is typically not permitted, so verify with the Cast Member), or simply say hi. These precious moments of connection are what make Disney character interactions so memorable.

Character Rotations: The characters who appear at each place usually rotate throughout the day. The Disneyland Paris app gives real-time information on which characters will welcome guests in certain areas, helping you to arrange your day more effectively.

Tips for a Magical Meet and Greet Experience: Planning is Key: Download the Disneyland Paris app and use the character locator to identify which characters will welcome guests at particular times and locations. This helps you to organize your meet-and-greets and avoid disappointment.
Do not forget your signature book and camera! Cast Members will frequently supply sticky stickers for signatures, ensuring that your treasured memories are saved.
Embrace the magic. Relax, have fun, and let your inner child come out! Disney characters are professionals at generating beautiful moments, so just enjoy the encounter and keep the memories in your heart.

Character Dining: A Deliciously Delightful Experience
Consider making a character dinner reservation at Walt Disney Studios Park for an unforgettable

eating experience. These delightful lunches allow you to share a scrumptious table with some of your favorite Disney characters, resulting in lasting memories of laughter, discussion, and, of course, great cuisine. Here's what to expect:

Designed Restaurants: Character eating experiences are available in wonderfully designed restaurants across the park. For example, Restaurant en Coulisses (Backstage Restaurant) has a delightful atmosphere inspired by a cartoon animator's workshop, whilst Auberge de Cendrillon (Cinderella's Inn) transports you to a storybook palace suited for a Princess. The setting enhances the eating experience.

Character Interactions: Throughout the lunch, iconic Disney characters will stop by your table for photographs, signatures, and pleasant discussion. These encounters offer an unforgettable eating experience, ideal for families with small children who want to share a meal with their favorite Disney heroes and princesses.

Delicious Cuisine: Character dining experiences provide a great variety of gastronomic possibilities.

Restaurant aux Coulisses serves classic French cuisine, while Plaza Gardens Restaurant serves international buffets. Make sure to review the menu selections ahead of time to ensure they meet your dietary needs and preferences.

Tips for Scheduling a Character Dining Experience

Reservations are key. Character dining experiences are quite popular, therefore making appointments well in advance is strongly advised. Reservations may be made online or by phone with Disneyland Paris Guest Services.

Choose your Experience: Walt Disney Studios Park provides a range of character dining experiences to suit different budgets and interests. When making your decision, think about the personalities you'd like to meet, the sort of cuisine you enjoy, and the general environment you want. Disneyland Paris is dedicated to supporting customers with dietary requirements. When booking your reservation, be sure to advise them of your needs, and Cast Members will gladly assist you in selecting appropriate alternatives and substitutes throughout your character eating experience. Here's an overview of the resources available to ensure a tasty and worry-free meal:

Disneyland Paris has a range of special dietary cuisines, including vegetarian, vegan, gluten-free, and alternatives for those who are allergic to peanuts, shellfish, and other common allergens. These menus can be obtained during your reservation or upon arrival at the restaurant.

Cast Member Knowledge: Cast Members at character eating establishments are taught to recognize and accommodate a variety of dietary requirements. Don't be afraid to share your special needs with them; they'll be pleased to walk you through the menu selections or confer with the chef to produce a personalized meal that suits your tastes.

Advanced Notice is Key: While Cast Members are pleased to accommodate last-minute requests, alerting them about your dietary requirements in advance helps them to plan properly. This promotes a more enjoyable eating experience and eliminates any potential delays.

Beyond Character Dining:
The focus on dietary needs goes beyond distinctive dining experiences. Here's what to anticipate at Walt Disney Studios Park:

Allergy Information on Menus: Most restaurants in Walt Disney Studios Park include allergy information on their menus. These symbols represent the presence of common allergies such as peanuts, gluten, soy, and milk.

Dietary Obtain Tags: Guests with food allergies may obtain a specific dietary request tag from Guest Services. This tag specifies your allergy limits and can be shown to Cast Members at any food and beverage place in the park.

Speaking with a Chef: In some situations, you may choose to talk with a chef to discuss your dietary requirements in further detail. Cast Members will be pleased to encourage this discourse, resulting in a personalized dining experience.

Planning Makes Perfect

Here are some helpful ideas for having a seamless and pleasurable eating experience at Walt Disney Studios Park:

Restaurant Options: Before you arrive, go over the menus at the park's many eateries. Disneyland Paris also offers a printable list of allergy-friendly alternatives on their website.

Download the Applications: The Disneyland Paris app allows you to filter restaurants based on your dietary requirements. This makes it easier to identify acceptable dining alternatives while you are visiting.

Pack Snacks: If you have certain dietary requirements that may not be met throughout the park, consider taking some snacks to ensure you have alternatives accessible.

Guests with dietary requirements may have a great and worry-free eating experience at Walt Disney Studios Park by following these suggestions and making use of the resources available. So, relax, taste the exquisite meals, and focus on making great memories throughout your Disney vacation!

Autograph Books and Photo Opportunities: Preserving Your Disney Memories Forever

Oh, the joy of a Disney character meeting! The thrill builds as you approach your favorite hero or princess. The anxious giggle before asking for an autograph. And the triumphant grin as you hold the autographed photo, a concrete reminder of your Disney dream come true. But, before you enter into the world of meet-and-greets and character eating, make sure you have the tools to keep these priceless experiences forever.

The Essential Autograph Book

Your autograph book is more than simply a collection of scribbles; it's a customized record of your Disney experience. Here's how to find the right one and make the most of it:

Size Matters: Think about mobility versus room for many signatures. A smaller, lighter book is better for carrying about the park, whilst a larger one allows for more elaborate messages or drawings from the characters.

Themed Magic: Make the encounter more memorable with a Disney-themed signing book. Find one with your favorite characters or movies for a sense of personality.

Acid-free Paper: Choose an autograph book with acid-free paper to keep your beloved autographs vivid for years.

Preparing for Perfection: Invest in high-quality pens that do not bleed through the paper. Choose thicker-tipped markers for characters with smaller hands.

Pro Tip for Autograph Success:

Get it Signed Early: Attend meet-and-greets during less busy periods for more comfortable contact and a better chance of receiving personalized remarks.

One book for each character. If you're going in a group, consider getting individual signing albums for each member. This allows the characters to personalize their signature, providing a more unique experience for everyone.

Be Polite and Patient: Characters interact with several guests during the day. Maintain courtesy and patience, and your pleasant vibe will show through.
Capture the Moment: Remember to take a photo with the character as they sign your autograph book!

Photographic Memories: Pose with Disney Royalty

Photos are another excellent method to preserve the magic of your Disney character interactions. Here's how you can obtain picture-perfect moments:

Camera Ready: Bring a trustworthy camera and a good flash to get excellent images in a variety of lighting settings. To prevent missing out, consider bringing a portable charger or additional batteries. The Power of Photos: Modern cell phones make taking photos with characters simple. Use a selfie stick to capture broader photos that incorporate the full background.
Embrace the Cast Members: Disney cast members are masters at capturing amazing moments. Don't be afraid to ask them to snap a

photo of you with your favorite character for a unique viewpoint.

Embrace the Background: Disney's fastidious attention to detail extends to character meet-and-greet areas. Use the vivid backdrops to create an immersive picture experience.

PhotoPass+ Advantages: Consider buying Disney PhotoPass+. This service permits professional photographers stationed throughout the park to document your character interactions and provide high-resolution downloads and prints.

Beyond the Autograph and Photograph:
The charm of a Disney character encounter is found in the interaction itself. Here are some extra suggestions to make the most of this unique occasion:

Dress the Part: Embrace your inner Disney fan! Wearing a Disney-themed attire can start conversations with the characters and improve the whole experience.

Do your research. Discover some fascinating facts about the character you're meeting. A simple "I loved your performance in [movie name]" or "Your dress is beautiful, just like in the movie!" may go a long way toward fostering a more personal connection.

Embrace the Unexpected: Disney characters might surprise you with a hug, a high five, or a lighthearted exchange. Be open to the unexpected and savor the unique moment.

Make a Memory: Let your inner kid show! Don't be scared to strike a ridiculous pose, laugh together, or simply enjoy meeting your favorite character. With a trusty autograph book, a camera, and a heart full of Disney enchantment, you're ready to record amazing memories of your character experiences at Disneyland Paris. So grab your signature book, strike a pose, and prepare to produce long-lasting memories that will make you grin for years!

Dazzling Entertainment and Shows: Spectacular Performances for All Ages

Walt Disney Studios Park is packed with exciting entertainment, including spectacular parades, heartfelt stage plays, and compelling character interactions. These live performances bring cherished Disney stories to life, encouraging spectators to enter fantasy realms, sing along to renowned songs, and experience Disney's magic come alive on stage. So grab your popcorn, take a comfy seat, and get ready to be carried away by the sparkling world of entertainment at Walt Disney Studios Park!

Disney Parades: A River of Enchantment Flows Down Main Street

The park's entertainment culture revolves around its enthralling parades. These lively processions wind their way down Hollywood Boulevard, converting the entire area into a stage for a stunning show of music, dancing, and Disney character appearances. Here's what to expect:

A Feast for the Senses: Disney parades provide a multisensory experience. Catchy music fills the air, vivid floats embellished with detailed embellishments pass by, and sparkling costumes sparkle in the sunlight. Characters come to life with dynamic dance routines and amusing interactions, producing an enthralling spectacle for audiences of all ages.

A Celebration of Disney Stories: Each parade has a unique theme, which generally honors renowned Disney stories or brands. You may find yourself transported to the enchanting realm of "Alice in Wonderland," enjoying a high-energy dance party with Mickey and his cronies, or perhaps going on a daring adventure with the brave heroes of Marvel Comics.

Prime Viewing Locations: Finding a good position to observe the procession is essential. Main Street, Hollywood Boulevard (from the Twilight Zone Tower of Terror™ to Animagique Theater), and several designated places near Studio 1 provide ideal viewing points. These places tend to fill up quickly, so arrive early to get a great location.

Parade Schedule: The parade schedule varies by season and day of the week. Check the Disneyland Paris app or park brochures for the most up-to-date parade schedule. This helps you to organize your day more efficiently and avoid missing out on this amazing show.

Tips For A Magical Parade Experience:
Grab a Park Map: A park map shows the parade route and allows you to plan your viewing area ahead of time.
Sunscreen and hats are vital for remaining comfortable in the Florida sun during parades, which usually take place in the afternoon.
Snacks and Drinks: Before the parade, consider getting some popcorn, snacks, or a refreshing drink. This guarantees that you have snacks to enjoy while watching the spectacular show.
Character Interactions: Keep a look out for wandering Disney characters before and after the parade. This is an excellent opportunity to take photographs and make lasting memories with your favorite Disney companions.

Live Stage Shows: A World of Wonders on Stage

Aside from the fascinating parades, Walt Disney Studios Park offers a range of live stage productions that bring famous Disney stories to life. These compelling presentations feature skilled actors, stunning costumes, and creative effects that send audiences on an amazing trip through the world of Disney enchantment. Here's a look at some of the park's most popular stage performances:

Mickey's PhilharMagic: This engaging 3D presentation transports you to a magnificent symphony hall with Mickey Mouse. Donald Duck plays the hapless conductor as legendary Disney scenarios are recreated in breathtaking 3D animation, complemented by a popular orchestral accompaniment. Prepare to be wowed by amazing effects, falling snow, and even a naughty Tinker Bell who sprinkles pixie dust throughout the auditorium. (Animagique Theater is located on Hollywood Boulevard at 48° 51 '23.2"N, 2° 27' 32.1"E).

Rhythm & Blues Mickey: Join Mickey Mouse and his naughty buddies for a high-energy musical adventure! This exciting concert includes toe-tapping songs, thrilling dance routines, and a tribute to rhythm and blues music. Prepare to clap along, sing your heart out, and feel the contagious energy of this riveting performance. (Location: Studio 1, Hollywood Boulevard, 48°51'23.2"N, 2°27'32.1"E).

Finding The Perfect Show:
With so many stage acts available throughout the day, it might be difficult to choose the best one. Here are some suggestions to help you decide:

Show Schedule and Duration: The Disneyland Paris app includes the show schedule and duration for each performance. This helps you to schedule your day more efficiently and prevent clashes with parades or character interactions.

Age Appropriateness: When picking a performance, consider your travel companions' ages and interests. Some programs are gearedbdesigned for younger audiences and featuring iconic Disney characters in a fanciful atmosphere. Others, like Moteurs...Action! The Stunt Show Spectacular (described below) may appeal more to thrill seekers due to its high-octane stunts and dangerous motorbike acts.

Show Summaries: The Disneyland Paris app and park booklets include summaries for each show. Before making your decision, go through these descriptions to get a feel for the plot, music style, and general mood.

Beyond the Stage: Captivating Entertainment Around the Park

Walt Disney Studios Park offers live entertainment in addition to parades and stage productions. Here are some additional appealing offerings you can find during your visit:

Disney Junior Live On Stage! This interactive presentation enables young attendees to sing, dance, and embark on a magical trip with their favorite Disney Junior characters.

Character Interactions: Throughout the park, there are dedicated areas where Disney characters meet and greet people. These heartfelt connections allow for photographs, signatures, and lasting memories.

Streetmosphere Performers: Keep an eye out for skilled street performers around the park. These performers, who range from jugglers and magicians to musicians and dancers, add to the park's enchanting and whimsical ambiance.

A World of Entertainment Awaits

The world of entertainment at Walt Disney Studios Park has something for everyone. From the brilliant spectacle of parades to the compelling stage plays and heartfelt character encounters, there's a performance that will captivate your attention and leave you with lasting memories. So grab your popcorn, take a comfy seat, and get ready to be carried away by the sparkling world of entertainment at Walt Disney Studios Park!

Nighttime Spectaculars: Illuminating the Sky with Fireworks and Storytelling

Nighttime Spectaculars: Illuminating the sky with fireworks and storytelling.

As the sun sets below the horizon at Walt Disney Studios Park, the magic takes on a new dimension. Prepare to be blown away by amazing nightly spectaculars that turn the park into a brilliant canvas of light, music, and storytelling. These breathtaking presentations blend stunning fireworks displays, engaging projections, and enticing music to create unique experiences that will leave you starry-eyed.

The Night Sky's Light Symphony
The breathtaking fireworks display is unquestionably the highlight of Walt Disney Studios Park's nighttime attractions. These spectacular shows combine cutting-edge technology to paint the night sky with vivid colors, stunning effects, and famous Disney artwork. Here's what to expect:

A Storytelling Spectacle: The fireworks display at Walt Disney Studios Park is more than just brilliant booms. They are precisely coordinated to present a compelling tale, frequently borrowing influence from popular Disney films and characters. Soar over the sky with Peter Pan, dive into the depths of the ocean with The Little Mermaid, or join the Avengers in an epic struggle for good, all brought to life by a stunning display of pyrotechnics and music.

A Multisensory Experience: Fireworks displays are more than simply a visual spectacle. They provide a multi-sensory experience that stimulates all of your senses. Thrilling music soars through the air, precisely coordinated with the colorful explosions in the sky. Lasers create beautiful patterns across the nocturnal landscape, while additional effects such as smoke and water cannons contribute to the show's mystical atmosphere.

Finding the Best Viewing Spot:
Finding a good place to observe the fireworks show is essential for making the most of your experience. Here are a few tips:

Center Plaza: This center hub provides a good view of the fireworks display, making it a popular watching area. However, it may become packed, so arriving early is advisable.
Studio 1: The area surrounding Studio 1 on Hollywood Boulevard is another great viewing place, but significantly less crowded than Central Plaza.
The Animation Courtyard offers a unique perspective on the fireworks display. While the view is somewhat obscured by buildings, it provides a picturesque location surrounded by Disney animation studios.

Nightly Spectaculars Schedule:
Fireworks displays are often held on peak season evenings, with showtimes varied based on the time of year. Check the Disneyland Paris app or park brochures for the most up-to-date schedule to avoid missing out on this spectacular show.

Tips For A Magical Nighttime Spectacular Experience
Grab a Snack: Before the performance, consider getting some popcorn, snacks, or a refreshing drink. This guarantees that you have snacks to enjoy as you watch the spectacular spectacle.
Bring a Blanket or Folding Chairs: If you want to arrive early for the fireworks show, consider bringing a blanket or folding chairs for extra comfort.
Dress for the Weather: Nighttime temperatures might drop significantly, so bring a light jacket or sweater to keep you warm throughout the event.

Beyond Fireworks: Enchanting Nighttime Entertainment

While fireworks are unquestionably the centerpiece of Walt Disney Studios Park's nightly spectaculars, additional engaging offers enhance the wonderful mood. Here are some other experiences to look forward to:

Illuminations: At night, the park's buildings and monuments come alive with dazzling lights and mesmerizing presentations. These illuminations convert the park into a sparkling fantasy, ideal for a promenade after the fireworks display.

Character Interactions: Certain character meet-and-greet sites stay open throughout the evening, allowing you to shoot photographs and enjoy a beautiful moment with your favorite Disney companions beneath a starry sky.

Dining with a View: Make a late supper reservation at a restaurant with a view of Central Plaza. This allows you to have a tasty lunch while watching the stunning fireworks show from the comfort of your table.

A Night to Remember

A trip to Walt Disney Studios Park isn't complete without witnessing the splendor of its nightly shows. The brilliant fireworks displays, engaging projections, and charming environment make for a genuinely unique event that will leave you with lifelong memories. So, gather your loved ones, find a great location, and be ready to be awestruck by the magnificence of a Disney evening spectacular!

Seasonal and Special Events Reveal the Magic Throughout the Year

Walt Disney Studios Park is more than simply a destination for thrill rides and character interactions; it's a lively environment that changes throughout the year with exciting seasonal and special events. These events enhance the excitement of your stay by providing exclusive experiences, themed décor, and special performances that honor festivals, cultural traditions, and classic Disney stories. So, regardless of when you arrive, there is always something fresh and fascinating to discover at Walt Disney Studios Park.

Celebration of Holidays:
Disney's Halloween Festival:

Every fall, the park changes into a hauntingly lovely refuge for Halloween fans. Spooky decorations cover the park, fun trick-or-treating possibilities emerge, and exciting Halloween-themed stage plays featuring Disney villains come to life. Don't forget to dress up in your favorite costume and enjoy the festivities!

Disney's Enchanted Christmas: As the year comes to an end, Walt Disney Studios Park celebrates the wonder of Christmas. A massive Christmas tree twinkles in Central Plaza, the park gleams with festive decorations, and heartfelt

Disney's Enchanted Christmas

Christmas concerts featuring popular Disney characters infuse the air with holiday spirit. Special parades featuring Disney characters dressed in their Christmas finest, as well as magical snowfall scenes, add to the holiday spirit.

Celebrate Cultural Traditions:

Disney Loves Jazz: Experience the world of jazz music during this exciting springtime event. Live jazz performances by skilled musicians fill the park with upbeat melodies, creating a lively and dynamic environment. Special character encounters with Disney companions dressed in their finest jazz gear, as well as specialized food and beverage selections, enhance the experience.

The Lion King & Timon's Hakuna Matata Jubilee: Celebrate the timeless story of "The Lion King" during this summer spectacle. The park is filled with vivid hues inspired by the African savanna, and thrilling stage acts starring favorite characters from the film bring the tale to life. This unique event includes special African-inspired food and beverage selections, as well as character encounters with Simba, Timon, and Pumbaa.

Special Events For All Ages:
Marvel Season of Heroes: Attention all superhero enthusiasts! This thrilling event honors the legendary heroes of the Marvel Universe. Witness thrilling feats starring renowned Marvel characters, take part in interactive challenges to put your superhero abilities to the test, and meet your favorite heroes in person for great picture opportunities.

The park is alive with Marvel-themed décor and unique food and beverage selections including superhero-inspired delights round out the experience.

Prepare for a galaxy adventure during Star Wars Season! Meet renowned characters like Chewbacca and Darth Vader, take part in thrilling Star Wars-themed activities, and watch stunning evening projections turn the park into a galaxy far, far away. This out-of-this-world event concludes with special food and beverage selections showcasing interplanetary goodies, as well as unique retail possibilities.

Tips for Planning a Visit to a Special Event:
Check the Calendar: Before deciding on your travel dates, visit the Disneyland Paris website or app to see the park's special events calendar. This allows you to base your visit on an event that piques your interest.

Book Early: Special activities at Walt Disney Studios Park tend to draw more attendees. Consider buying your park tickets and hotel accommodations well in advance, especially if you're visiting during high season.

Themed Attire: On some special occasions, park attendees are encouraged to dress in theme. Pack clothing that represents the spirit of the event you'll be attending, enhancing the whole experience.

A Year-round Celebration of Magic

Walt Disney Studios Park has a full calendar of seasonal and special events throughout the year, so there's always something new and interesting to explore. There's something for everyone, from eerie Halloween parties to touching Christmas gatherings, and from thrilling superhero experiences to interstellar Star Wars encounters. So, pack your bags, release your inner kid, and get ready to enjoy the enchantment of Walt Disney Studios Park no matter the season!

A Gastronomical Adventure: Dining Delights in Disneyland Paris

Fueling up for a day of exhilarating rides, engaging shows, and heartfelt character interactions is an important element of any Disneyland Paris visit. While getting a fast lunch on the run is easy, sometimes you want a more nuanced and immersive eating experience.

This is where Walt Disney Studios Park's table-service restaurants come in. These elegantly designed restaurants provide an unforgettable gastronomic trip, taking you to mythical realms while tempting your taste buds with scrumptious meals and outstanding service. So, relax your belts and get ready for a culinary trip through some of Walt Disney Studios Park's best table-service restaurants!

Table-Service Restaurants Provide Fine-Dining Experiences fit for Royalty

Table-service restaurants provide a more leisurely and sophisticated eating experience than quick-service choices. Here's what to expect:

Immersive Theming: Each table-service restaurant has its theme, carefully developed to bring you to the heart of a great Disney story. Dine in the luxury of Hollywood's Golden Age at Hollywood Tower Restaurant, or take a gourmet journey through the busy streets of New York City at Manhattan Restaurant. The immersive setting adds another dimension of charm to your eating experience.

Table-Side Service: Compared to quick-service restaurants, table-service venues provide a more individualized eating experience. A specialized waiter will walk you through the menu, answer any questions you may have, and make your dining experience nothing short of amazing.

Multi-Course Meals: Table-service restaurants usually serve multi-course meals, which allow you to sample a range of gastronomic delicacies. These meals include appetizers, main dishes, desserts, and beverages, making for a comprehensive and gratifying eating experience.

Choosing the Best Table-Service Restaurant:
Walt Disney Studios Park has a broad assortment of table-service restaurants that appeal to a variety of interests and preferences. Here are some aspects to consider before making your decision:

Theme: Consider the restaurant's theme and whether it matches your hobbies. Do you want a dazzling Hollywood experience or a taste of traditional Americana? Choosing a restaurant that fits your Disney trip theme will improve your whole experience.

Cuisine: Each restaurant has a separate menu that includes a range of cuisines. Whether you want classic French dining, trendy American cuisine, or Italian delights, there is a restaurant to satisfy your cravings.

Budget: Table-service eating experiences are often more expensive than quick-service ones. Consider your budget while making your decision, and keep in mind the cost of beverages as well as any prospective character eating experiences.

A Spotlight on Culinary Delights:
Here's a look at some of the most popular table-service restaurants at Walt Disney Studios Park, giving you a taste of the wonderful delights that await:

Hollywood Tower Restaurant (located on Hollywood Boulevard at 48°51'23.2"N, 2°27'32.1"E): Dine in a perfectly replicated Hollywood Tower Hotel atmosphere. The restaurant's menu offers classic American cuisine with a contemporary touch, such as delectable steaks, luscious seafood dishes, and indulgent desserts. Keep an eye out for unique character dining experiences with Disney villains, which will bring an added element of fun to your dinner.

Bistrot Chez Rémy (48°51'24.0"N, 2°27'34.2"E): Shrink down to the size of Remy, the brave rat chef from "Ratatouille," and dine amongst the bustling kitchen of Gusteau's restaurant. This lovely Parisian-style café serves a delectable menu of French delicacies, with fresh seasonal ingredients and superb presentation.

Plan Your Table-Service Dining Experience
Here are some useful ideas for a seamless and pleasurable table-service eating experience:

Reservations: Reservations are strongly advised, particularly during busy seasons and at popular restaurants. You may make reservations online or by calling the Disneyland Paris reservation service.
Dress Code: Although there is no official dress code at Walt Disney Park table-service restaurants, smart casual clothes are often preferred.

Dietary Restrictions: Walt Disney Studios Park caters to a variety of dietary requirements. Please notify your waiter of any allergies or dietary restrictions you may have, and they will gladly assist you in selecting appropriate alternatives from the menu or consulting with the chef to create a personalized meal.

Beyond the Table: The World of Culinary Delights

Walt Disney Studios Park has a wide range of culinary options beyond table-service restaurants to satisfy appetites and quench thirst throughout the day. Here's a look at some of the other options you'll find:

Quick-Service Restaurants: For a quick and easy meal, the park has various quick-service restaurants that serve a range of cuisines. From basic American favorites like burgers and fries to Asian-inspired meals and refreshing salads, you'll be able to fulfill your appetites while on the road. These restaurants use counter service, which means you order your food and beverages at a dedicated counter and then sit down to eat.

Snack Bars & Kiosks: Snack bars and kiosks are located around the park, offering tantalizing food and beverages. On a hot summer day, enjoy a delicious scoop of ice cream, a toasty Mickey-shaped pretzel, or a cold drink. These simple solutions are ideal for a fast energy boost while exploring the park.

Character Dining: For a memorable dining experience, try reserving a character meal. These unique dinners allow you to dine with your favorite Disney characters, creating unforgettable experiences for guests of all ages. Character encounters, picture ops, and signatures are usually included in the dinner package, making it a spectacular chance to reconnect with your favorite Disney friends.

Tips for a Delicious Day at the Park:
Plan Your Meals: Having a basic concept of where you want to dine ahead of time will help you save time browsing for possibilities.
Mobile Ordering: The Disneyland Paris app allows you to order food and beverages from certain quick-service restaurants. This might be a time-saving choice, particularly during peak lunch and supper periods.
Portion Sizes: Consider sharing meals, particularly with small children. Table-service restaurants can

provide big portions, and sharing allows you to try a broader range of foods without breaking the bank.

Budgeting: Create a budget for your meals and snacks ahead of time. This allows you to keep in control of your spending and prevent unforeseen expenses.

A World of Flavors Awaits

Walt Disney Studios Park has everything for everyone's taste buds and eating preferences, from beautiful table-service dinners to efficient quick-service alternatives and delicious snacks on the move. So, be ready to go on a wonderful gastronomic trip as you explore the park's many offers. With a little forethought and some helpful hints, you can make your dining experiences at Walt Disney Studios Park as spectacular as the rest of your trip!

Quick-Service Restaurants: Fueling Your Adventures with Delicious Food

Walt Disney Studios Park welcomes travelers of all tastes! You'll get hungry in between exhilarating rides, enthralling performances, and touching character interactions. Fortunately, the park has a broad selection of quick-service eateries that are ideal for getting a good snack on the run while maintaining flavor and enjoyment.

A World of Cuisines at Your Fingertips
These quick cafés serve a variety of cuisines, guaranteeing that there is something to fulfill every need. Here's an idea of what you may expect:

Classic American Favorites: Do you crave a juicy burger or a basket of golden fries? Look no further! Several quick-service restaurants specialize in American comfort cuisine, which is ideal for a hearty and familiar dinner.
International Flavors: Experience a global gastronomic excursion without leaving the park. There are plenty of options for Asian-inspired foods like noodles and stir-fries, Mexican delicacies

like tacos and burritos, and Italian staples like spaghetti and pizza.

Healthy Options: For health-conscious park goers, various quick-service eateries serve lighter fare such as fresh salads, wraps, and grilled foods. You won't have to sacrifice flavor for a nutritious and fulfilling supper.

Convenience is Key

The quick-service eateries at Walt Disney Studios Park are created with convenience in mind. Here's what to expect:

Counter Service: Simply approach the relevant counter, peruse the menu above, and place your order with a kind Cast Member. They would be pleased to answer any queries you may have regarding the menu selections.

Quick Service: The emphasis is on quickness and effectiveness. Orders are produced fresh and delivered quickly, allowing you to spend less time waiting and more time visiting the park's various activities.

Most quick-service restaurants have both indoor and outdoor seating options. Choose a comfy area to eat, people-watch, or take in the colorful park environment.

Make the Most of Your Quick-Service Experience

Here are some useful ideas to make your quick-service eating experience easy and enjoyable:

Mobile Ordering: Download the Disneyland Paris app and use the mobile ordering option. Browse menus, place orders, and pay immediately from the app, saving you important time waiting in line. When your order is ready, simply pick it up at one of the authorized counters.

Sharing is Caring: Quick-service restaurants might serve substantial portions, particularly for small children. Consider sharing meals to save money and sample a larger range of foods.

Dietary Restrictions: Walt Disney Studios Park aims to meet a variety of dietary needs. Look for allergy information on the menu, or ask a Cast Member about gluten-free, vegetarian, or vegan alternatives. They'll be pleased to help you identify suitable options.

Beyond The Meal:
Quick-service restaurants offer more than simply food; they also provide a pleasant and interactive dining experience. Here's what you may encounter:

Theming: Many quick-service restaurants include themes that complement neighboring attractions. For example, have a nibble at "Animagique Café" in a delightful Parisian setting, or recharge with a quick supper at "Studio Catering Co.", which is inspired by a vintage Hollywood studio set.
Character Encounters: Keep a look out for unexpected character sightings at specified quick-service outlets throughout the park. Taking a selfie or obtaining an autograph from your favorite Disney character adds a wonderful touch to your dining experience.

Fueling Your Adventures

The quick-service eateries at Walt Disney Studios Park are ideal for stopping to refresh and refuel in between the park's various activities. With a wide variety of cuisines, handy service choices, and a touch of Disney enchantment, you're sure to discover a quick-service restaurant that will satisfy your cravings and keep you energetic for a day of wonderful park activities.

Character Dining: Sharing a Meal and Memories with Favorite Characters

The opportunity to engage with cherished characters is often seen as a highlight of every Disney visit. Character dining experiences at Walt Disney Studios Park elevate the experience to new heights. These delightful dinners allow you to dine with some of your favorite Disney buddies, resulting in unforgettable experiences that will be treasured for years.

Imagineering Magic: A World Where Stories Come to Life

The character dining restaurants at Walt Disney Studios Park are beautifully designed, bringing you to the heart of a famous Disney story. Here's what to expect:

Immersive Atmosphere: Enter a universe inspired by classic Disney films. Dine in the busy streets of New York City with Mickey and his buddies at "Restaurant en Coulisse," or go on an underwater adventure with Nemo and Dory at "Bistrot Chez Rémy" (a table-service restaurant that offers character dining experiences on certain days). The immersive surroundings provide an extra dimension of charm to your meal.

Meet and Greet Opportunities: The main draw of character dining is, of course, the opportunity to engage with favorite Disney characters. Throughout your lunch, Disney characters will stop by your table for photographs, signatures, and fun conversation. This personalized contact enables you to make memorable memories with your favorite Disney friends.

Choosing the Perfect Character Dining Experience

Walt Disney Studios Park provides a range of character dining experiences, each with a unique character and location. Here are some aspects to consider before making your decision:

Characters: Is there a Disney character you'd desire to meet? Choose a character dining experience that includes your favorites. Popular choices include Mickey and his buddies, Disney princesses, and Marvel superheroes.

Setting: Consider the restaurant's concept and whether it matches your hobbies. Do you want a classic Disney experience or a contemporary Marvel-inspired setting?

Meal Type: Character dining experiences are normally available for breakfast, lunch, and supper. Select a meal time that corresponds to your schedule and preferences.

Making the Most of Your Character Dining Experience

Here are some ways to make your character's eating experience spectacular and unforgettable:

Reservations: Character dining experiences are extremely popular and book up quickly. Make bookings well in advance of your visit, particularly during high seasons.

Dress Requirement: While there is no particular dress requirement, smart casual clothes are often preferred. Some character-eating events may require themed dress, so check ahead if you want to partake.

Capture the Moment: Bring your camera or phone to take photographs and videos of your encounters with Disney characters.

Relax and Enjoy: The most essential thing is to unwind and enjoy your experience. Allow the Disney enchantment to wash over you and create unforgettable moments with your loved ones.

A Touch of Disney Magic

Character dining experiences at Walt Disney Studios Park provide an amazing opportunity to interact with your favorite Disney characters. These unique meals will become cherished memories of your Disney visit, with heartwarming encounters and great images, as well as wonderful cuisine and an immersive ambiance. So, make your reservation, put on a grin, and get ready to get carried away by the enchantment of character dining!

Shopping Spree at Disneyland Paris' Enchanting Boutiques

The excitement of a Disney visit wouldn't be complete without a memento or two (or 10) to remember the great recollections. Disneyland Paris satisfies this need with a stunning selection of charming stores located throughout the park and Disney Village. Whether you're looking for the perfect cuddly toy for a young one, a trendy T-shirt to show off your Disney devotion, or a limited-edition collectible for the serious fan, there's a treasure trove of delights waiting to be discovered. So put on your metaphorical shopping shoes and join us for a whirlwind tour of Disneyland Paris' intriguing shopping environment!

Discovering the Perfect Souvenir: Toys, Apparel, and Collectibles

For Young Adventurers: A World of Plush and Playthings (48°52′29″ N, 2°31′59″ E)

When you go into one of the parks' many stores, you will be met with a symphony of color and cuddly friends. The shelves are packed with Disney plush toys, including the famous Mickey Mouse and Minnie Mouse, as well as renowned characters from newer flicks such as Moana and Frozen. For young children, these soft pals become treasured companions throughout the journey, providing comfort during character meet-and-greets and prompting imaginative play during downtime. Look for soft toys in a range of sizes, suitable for cuddling or exhibiting.

Beyond the plush sanctuary, the stores provide a fascinating selection of items ideal for igniting imaginations and reliving cherished Disney stories. Action figures, playsets, construction sets, and even interactive cuddly toys with sound effects bring beloved characters to life, allowing kids to imagine their own wonderful experiences. Don't forget to check out the character-themed board games and puzzles, which are a great way to spend quality time together after a day of exploring the park.

Fashionable Fairytale: Apparel for All Ages (48°52′29″N, 2°31′59″E)
Disneyland Paris does not disappoint when it comes to clothing and accessories, with a diverse collection for all ages and types. Whether you're a die-hard Disney fan or simply want a touch of whimsy in your clothing, you'll find something to suit your taste.

For the smaller ones, there are lovely character-themed clothes showcasing everyone from traditional princesses to endearing Pixar characters. Look for cute skirts, comfortable t-shirts, warm sweatshirts, and fun accessories like caps, backpacks, and sunglasses featuring their favorite characters.

Adults may also join in on the excitement! The parks provide a trendy range of t-shirts, sweatshirts, and hats with famous Disney emblems and character designs. Consider wearing a spirit jersey, which is a comfy, long-sleeved shirt with a character silhouette on the back and park emblems on the sleeves. Spirit jerseys are a popular option among

Disney fans and are available in a range of colors and character designs.

A Collector's Paradise: Limited-Edition Treasures (48°52′29″ N, 2°31′59″ E)

For true Disney fans, Disneyland Paris has a collection of limited-edition memorabilia that are guaranteed to become valued belongings. These unique objects might range from wonderfully crafted pins with elaborate artwork to character miniatures molded with careful precision. Many collectibles are released to commemorate important events or anniversaries, making them even more valuable to devoted fans.

If you're looking for a limited-edition treasure, visit stores near park entrances and in Disney Village. These stores often feature a special area displaying the most recent releases. Remember, great items frequently sell out, so don't wait if something strikes your eye!

Beyond the Basics: Themed Boutiques and Hidden Gems (48°52′29″ N, 2°31′59″ E)
While the stores described above have an excellent selection of items, Disneyland Paris also has several specialized boutiques that appeal to certain interests. For example, Star Wars enthusiasts may visit a specialized shop at Walt Disney Studios Park, which sells lightsabers, character gear, and memorabilia from a galaxy far, far away. Marvel fans may gather in the Marvel Zone in Disney Village to purchase superhero-themed clothes, figurines, and accessories.

For those looking for something different, visit the stores on Main Street, U.S.A. at Disneyland Park. These lovely businesses provide a great selection of vintage-inspired gifts. The Chapeau Rouge (Red Hat) sells vintage Disney-themed headwear, while Main Street Motors displays car-themed items and nostalgic Disney memorabilia.

Enchanting Extras include Practical Souvenirs and Disney Magic

The fascinating world of Disneyland Paris shopping goes beyond plush toys, apparel, and memorabilia. Here are some extra gems you may uncover during your shopping spree:

Practical Magic: Don't forget the necessities! Shops throughout the park sell practical items to help you remember your experience. Think Mickey Mouse-shaped water bottles to stay hydrated, fashionable phone covers with your favorite characters, and fun-designed rain ponchos to keep you dry in unexpected showers.

Disney PhotoPass Goods: Capture your amazing experiences forever with a range of Disney PhotoPass goods available at certain locations. Choose from beautiful frames, fun-shaped keychains, and even digital downloads to display your Disney images.

Earp-Tastic Fun: A Disney visit is not complete without the famous Mickey Mouse ears! Shops across the park sell a dazzling assortment of these popular headbands in a variety of designs, colors, and character themes. Find traditional Minnie Mouse ears with polka dots, light-up versions for nighttime outings, and character-specific designs ranging from Spider-Man to Elsa.

Pin Trading: For a one-of-a-kind and engaging keepsake experience, explore the world of Disney pin trading. Many businesses sell character-themed pins, which you may collect, trade, or just admire for their detailed patterns. Pin swapping with other Disney fans adds a social element and fun to your souvenir quest.

Sweet Snacks: Satisfy your sweet appetite with delicious Disney-themed snacks available at select shops and kiosks. These sugary keepsakes, ranging from Mickey Mouse-shaped lollipops to chocolate delicacies depicting your favorite characters, are a fun way to remember your vacation while also satisfying your sweet tooth.

Shopping with Ease: Maximizing Your Retail Therapy

Disneyland Paris aims to make your shopping experience as smooth and pleasurable as possible. Here are some useful ideas for maximizing your retail therapy session:

Planning Your Itinerary: With so many stores around the parks and Disney Village, it's a good idea to plan your shopping itinerary ahead of time. Park maps often emphasize the location of key stores, helping you to organize your shopping trips to avoid retracing. Consider using the Disneyland Paris app to view interactive maps and filter stores by category (for example, apparel, toys, and collectibles).

Taking Advantage of Services: Disneyland Paris provides a handy shopping bag pickup service. Simply pick up your purchases at specified spots around the parks and return them at the end of the day at the Main Street, U.S.A. exit in Disneyland Park or the World of Disney shop in Disney Village.

This allows you to spend the day exploring the park without having to carry heavy shopping bags.

Tax-Free Shopping: Non-EU residents may be entitled to a VAT refund on their purchases. Look for stores with the "Tax-Free Shopping" badge. Make careful to ask about the procedure and get the relevant papers at the place of purchase.

Budgeting: Souvenirs might be tempting, so make a budget before your vacation. This can help you avoid overpaying and return home with wonderful memories and reasonable credit card expenses. Consider setting aside a particular amount for souvenirs and sharing it with your vacation buddies, if applicable.

A Final Touch of Enchantment: Memories for a Lifetime

As you explore Disneyland Paris' lovely stores, keep in mind that the actual treasures you'll find go beyond plush animals and character t-shirts. It's the joy shared with loved ones on exhilarating rides, the breathtaking amazement of watching a spectacular sight, and the sweet memories you make together.

Make your buying spree an extension of that magic, a way to remember the excitement and wonder of your Disney visit. So go out, explore the enthralling world of Disneyland Paris shopping, and choose the ideal gifts to take a bit of the enchantment home with you!

Themed Merchandise: Bring a Piece of the Magic Home (48°52′29″ N, 2°31′59″ E)

Disneyland Paris takes the notion of themed stuff to the next level, including tale and character characteristics in every item. Aside from the traditional character t-shirts and soft toys, the park has a treasure trove of souvenirs meant to bring you back to your favorite Disney stories and experiences. Here's a look at some of the fascinating themed goods you may find:

Adventureland: Prepare for Exploration

Enter Adventureland and immerse yourself in a world of brave adventurers and secret riches. The shops here are brimming with items inspired by great films such as Indiana Jones and Pirates of the Caribbean. Think Indiana Jones-inspired fedoras and khaki vests, ideal for channeling your inner archaeologist. Aspiring pirates may get eye patches, pirate caps, and even toy copies of Captain Jack Sparrow's compass. Interactive maps and treasure hunt kits provide another element of excitement, allowing kids to go on their pirate adventures across the park.

Frontierland: A Collection of Rootin' Tootin' Goods

Frontierland transports you back to the Wild West, and the goods capture that essence. Wear cowboy hats, sheriff badges, and bandanas fit for a dusty saloon. For small ones, adorable clothes portraying Woody, Jessie, and the rest of the Toy Story team evoke the land's fun spirit. Look for entertaining home décor pieces like wooden signs with famous Disney character phrases or small copies of renowned Frontierland features such as the Big Thunder Mountain Railroad.

Fantasyland: Where Fairytales Come to Life!
Fantasyland is the land of princesses, castles, and happily ever after. The shops here are packed with products inspired by timeless classics such as Cinderella, Sleeping Beauty, and Beauty and the Beast. With lovely costumes, tiaras, and dazzling accessories, children may dress up as their favorite princesses. Adults may find gorgeous scarves, jewelry, and homeware products with delicate floral designs and fairytale motifs. Don't miss the plush doll collection featuring renowned Disney princesses and their animal companions.

Discoveryland: Souvenirs From the Future
Step into the future at Discoveryland and experience a realm of innovation and cosmic adventure. The stores here sell goods inspired by popular films such as Star Wars and Buzz Lightyear. Channel your inner Jedi Knight with lightsabers, character t-shirts with classic motifs from a galaxy far, far away, and even droid-themed phone covers.

Buzz Lightyear action toys, jetpack backpacks, and glow-in-the-dark stars bearing the Space Ranger emblem are available to aspiring space rangers. Interactive toys and science-themed kits inspire youngsters to discover the marvels of space and technology.

Walt Disney Studios Park - Lights, Camera, Action!

Walt Disney Studios Park commemorates the wonder of filmmaking and animation. The stores here sell products inspired by popular Disney and Pixar films, ranging from the roaring twenties splendor of Mickey's PhilharMagic to the magical world of Cars. Pose with Mickey Mouse ears that depict memorable movie sequences, or harness your inner superhero with Marvel Studios character-themed t-shirts and accessories. For Pixar fans, there are charming plushies representing characters from Finding Nemo and Toy Story, as well as painting tools and sketchbooks to inspire your creative activities.

A Touch of Disney Magic for Each Fan

The capacity to cater to every taste and interest is what makes Disneyland Paris' themed products so appealing. Whether you're a die-hard Star Wars fan, a princess enthusiast, or just a fan of old Disney stories, you'll find something to take you back to your favorite moments in the park. So, enjoy the spirit of adventure, rediscover the charm of narrative, and bring home a piece of Disney enchantment with each themed memento you select.

Adventures in Paris: Exploring the City of Lights

Paris, the City of Lights, entices visitors with its timeless elegance, rich history, and renowned buildings. A vacation to Disneyland Paris isn't complete unless you go outside the park gates and experience the beauty of this mesmerizing town. This chapter serves as your guide to must-see attractions, providing thorough information and practical advice for planning fantastic day excursions from Disneyland Paris.

Day Trip 1: Reaching for the Sky—A Visit to the Eiffel Tower

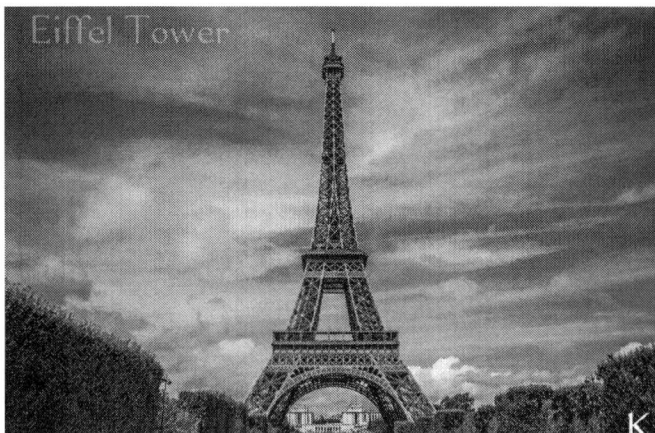

The Eiffel Tower, the indisputable icon of Paris, pierces the Parisian skyline with its wrought-iron lattice work that rises 324 meters (1,063 feet) into the air. Gustave Eiffel's visionary masterpiece, built for the 1889 World's Fair, continues to wow tourists with its spectacular views and architectural marvels.

Location and Getting There:
The Eiffel Tower is situated in the Champ de Mars (48°51′29″N, 2°29′47″E), a large public park in Paris' 7th district. The Eiffel Tower is easily

accessible from Disneyland Paris. Here are the
options:

RER Train: The RER A line begins at
Marne-la-Vallée station (which serves Disneyland
Paris) and brings you directly to Charles de
Gaulle-Étoile station (Arc de Triomphe), a
10-minute walk from the Eiffel Tower. The trip
takes around 40 minutes.
Taxi: Although somewhat more expensive, a taxi
provides a convenient and straightway from
Disneyland Paris to the Eiffel Tower. The travel
duration can vary based on traffic conditions, but
expect it to take between 45 and 60 minutes.

Ticketing and Visits:
Tickets to the Eiffel Tower can be purchased online
in advance or at the ticket kiosks located at the
tower's base. There are many ticket alternatives
available, allowing you to ascend to different levels:

The second floor provides breathtaking panoramic
views of the city, ideal for capturing those
picture-perfect moments.

Summit: For the very daring, climb to the very top of the Eiffel Tower for unequaled, spectacular views of Paris. Keep in mind that seats to the summit frequently sell out, so buying online in advance is highly encouraged.

A Towering Experience:
A visit to the Eiffel Tower involves more than just going to the top. Here's what to expect:

Before heading to the tower, take a stroll along the Champ de Mars. Picnic on the wide meadows, take in the Parisian ambiance or watch the breathtaking Eiffel Tower from afar.
Interactive exhibitions: The base of the tower features interactive exhibitions about the Eiffel Tower's history and construction. Learn about the architectural wonder that created this famous skyscraper, as well as its historical significance in Paris.
Restaurants: Several restaurants are located on the Eiffel Tower's various floors, ranging from simple cafés to fine-dining experiences with panoramic city

views. Enjoy a fantastic supper in a genuinely unique Parisian setting.

Day Trip 2: Discovering Artistic Treasures - Exploring the Louvre Museum

At the Louvre Museum, you may step back in time and immerse yourself in the world's best art collection. Located in the center of Paris (48°51'46"N, 2°36'45"E), this huge palace-turned-museum exhibits treasures from eras and civilizations. From the enigmatic Mona Lisa to the breathtaking Venus de Milo, the Louvre provides an unrivaled creative experience.

Plan Your Visit:

The Louvre Museum is large, so organizing your visit ahead of time is essential. The official museum website offers downloadable maps and highlights sections, allowing you to prioritize artworks that catch your interest. Here are some more tips:

Tickets can be purchased online in advance to prevent long lines, particularly during busy seasons.

Opening Hours: The Louvre is usually open from 9:00 a.m. to 6:00 p.m., with extended hours on select weekdays. Before visiting the museum, double-check the website for the most up-to-date operating hours.

Consider arranging a guided tour, especially if you have limited time or specific interests. A qualified guide can explore the large museum and give information about the artworks and their makers.

A World of Artistic Delight:
The Louvre Museum holds a massive collection organized into eight curatorial sections. Here's a look at some of the museum's highlights:

Department of Egyptian Antiquities: Travel through ancient Egypt and marvel at mummies, sarcophagi, and lavishly decorated statues of pharaohs, deities, and ordinary people. This extensive collection provides insight into the intriguing culture that existed along the Nile River for millennia.

Department of Near Eastern Antiquities:
Discover the artistic legacy of Mesopotamia, Persia, and the Levant. Admire exquisite Mesopotamian cylinder seals, massive Assyrian reliefs, and breathtaking Babylonian artifacts that convey the history of these ancient civilizations.

Department of Greek and Roman Antiquities:
Immerse yourself in classical culture and see Greece and Rome's creative legacy. Admire the fine details of Roman sarcophagi and ceramics, as well as classic sculptures such as the Venus de Milo and the Winged Victory of Samothrace.

The Department of Paintings holds the Louvre's crown treasures, including the world-famous Mona Lisa by Leonardo da Vinci. Explore galleries including masterpieces by Renaissance painters such as Raphael and Titian, marvel at the Dutch Golden Age with works by Rembrandt and Vermeer, and discover French classics by Delacroix and Ingres.

Beyond the Masterpieces:
The Louvre Museum provides more than simply a collection of world-famous artworks. What else can you experience?

The Louvre Palace: The museum itself is a historical treasure. Explore the luxurious palace suites, marvel at the great architecture, and see the delicate details that tell the story of the French monarchy.

The Tuileries Garden: Adjacent to the Louvre is the stunning Tuileries Garden, a spacious public park ideal for a stroll or picnic lunch. Soak in the Parisian ambiance, observe the manicured gardens and statues, and take a break from the city's bustling activity.

Temporary Exhibitions: The Louvre Museum regularly holds temporary exhibitions that highlight certain artists, historical periods, or artistic movements. Check the museum's website to see if any current exhibitions interest you.

A Parisian Treasure Trove:
The Louvre Museum represents humanity's artistic achievements throughout time and civilizations. A visit allows you to dig into the heart of art history, see masterpieces up close, and develop a better grasp of the world's cultural legacy. Prepare to be astonished as you begin this incredible creative journey!

Day Trip Options Abound:
Aside from the Eiffel Tower and the Louvre Museum, there are several additional day trip options in Paris. Here are some ideas based on your interests:

For History Lovers: Discover the majesty of the Palace of Versailles, a former royal home that exudes French wealth and splendor.
For Art Enthusiasts: Walk through the picturesque Montmartre area, a famous artists' paradise, and visit the Sacré-Coeur church, which offers stunning city vistas.
For Thrill Seekers: Visit Parc Astérix, a thrilling amusement park featuring roller coasters, themed

attractions, and performances based on the popular Astérix comic book characters.

Planning Your Parisian Adventure:
To guarantee a seamless and pleasurable experience during your Disneyland Paris day visits, consider these tips:

Purchase a Paris Visite Pass: This simple pass provides unlimited access to public transportation throughout Paris, including the metro, buses, and the RER trains.

Pack Light: Comfortable shoes are essential for exploring the city on foot. Consider taking a reusable water bottle and a small bag to transport supplies.

Learn a Few French words: While English is often spoken in tourist destinations, a few simple French words such as "Bonjour" (hello), "Merci" (thank you), and "Parlez-vous Anglais?" (Do you speak English?) may go a long way toward demonstrating respect for local culture.

A Parisian Adventure Awaits

Paris, with its famous sites, world-renowned museums, and compelling ambiance, guarantees a memorable visit. Use this chapter as a guide to begin a quest of exploration around the City of Light! Remember, these day trips just scratch the surface of what Paris has to offer. So tie up your walking shoes, enjoy the Parisian atmosphere, and make memories that last a lifetime.

Parisian Delights: Indulge in French Cuisine and Cultural Experiences

Beyond the excitement of Disneyland Paris is another world waiting to be discovered: the intriguing city of Paris. A vacation to the "City of Lights" would be incomplete without immersing oneself in its rich cultural tapestry and, of course, sampling the exquisite delights of French gastronomy. This chapter is your guide to discovering the finest of Parisian food and cultural offers, transforming your visit into a multi-sensory journey.

A Culinary Journey: Discovering the Flavors of France

French cuisine is known for its use of fresh, seasonal ingredients, immaculate presentation, and a focus on providing a balanced and enjoyable dining experience. Here's how to plan your Parisian gastronomic adventure:

Fine-Dining Experiences: Paris has a multitude of Michelin-starred restaurants that provide magnificent multi-course meals created by culinary experts. While these places are expensive, they provide a memorable gastronomic adventure for those with discriminating tastes.

Charming Bistros: The heart of Parisian food is found in its charming bistros. These little neighborhood jewels provide a more relaxed dining experience, focusing on classic French delicacies such as boeuf bourguignon (beef Burgundy stew) and coq au vin (chicken in wine). The environment is usually lively and hospitable, making it ideal for learning about the local culture.

Hidden Jewels: Venture beyond the tourist destinations to find hidden jewels nestled away on charming Parisian alleys. These smaller, family-run restaurants can provide a more genuine experience, with traditional cuisine handed down through generations.

Must-try Parisian Dishes:
No Paris gastronomic vacation is complete without trying some of the city's iconic dishes. Here are some ideas to stimulate your taste buds:

Croissants and Pain au Chocolat: For the traditional Parisian breakfast, try a flaky, buttery croissant or a pain au chocolat, which is a croissant filled with rich dark chocolate. For the ultimate Parisian morning routine, pair these pleasures with a cup of strong coffee.

Soupe à l'Oignon Gratinée: Warm your soul with a hot bowl of French onion soup, a substantial broth rich in caramelized onions and topped with a golden-brown crust of melted cheese.

Steak-Frites: Enjoy the simplicity of properly cooked steak served with crunchy French fries. This traditional meal is a mainstay on many Parisian restaurant menus and is sure to please.

Macarons: These delicate pastries are both visually appealing and delicious. Macarons come in a variety of flavors, ranging from conventional vanilla and chocolate to more unusual selections like rose and pistachio. They are a delicious treat to enjoy with a cup of tea or coffee.

Beyond the Plate: A Cultural Feast of the Senses

Paris has a multitude of cultural events that complement its gastronomic culture. Here are a few ways to go deeper into the city's unique cultural tapestry:

Museums: From the world-renowned Louvre Museum, which houses famous treasures such as the Mona Lisa, to more specialized museums such as the Musée Picasso, which showcases Pablo Picasso's works, Paris has something for everyone.

Walking Tours: Take a guided walking tour led by an experienced local who may give intriguing insights into Paris' history, architecture, and hidden treasures.

Wine Tastings: Experience the world of French wine during a wine-tasting session. Learn about grape varietals, locations, and pairings to find your new favorite French wine.

Opéra Garnier: Experience the grandeur of Parisian opera at the Palais Garnier, a majestic opera theater renowned for its sumptuous architecture and world-class performances.

Accept the Parisian Art de Vivre (Art of Living):

Parisian culture is all about enjoying the little things in life. Here are some methods to experience Paris' "art de vivre" during your visit:

Picnic in a Parisian Park: Purchase fresh bread, cheese, charcuterie, and a bottle of wine from a local market before enjoying a leisurely picnic lunch in a lovely Parisian park such as the Jardin du Luxembourg or the Champ de Mars.

People-Watching at a Café: Sit at a gorgeous outside café, drink an espresso or a glass of wine, and watch the dynamic Parisian life unfold in front of you.

Explore Local Markets: Experience the sights, sounds, and fragrances of a Parisian market. Stroll among vendors full of fresh fruit, handmade cheeses, and local delights.

Browse Quirky Stores: Wander through the lovely alleyways of the Marais or Saint-Germain-des-Prés to uncover one-of-a-kind stores highlighting French fashion, art, and design.

Plan Your Parisian Adventure:
For a seamless and pleasurable Parisian gastronomic and cultural experience, consider these factors for a seamless and pleasurable Parisian food and cultural experience:

Learning a Few simple French words: While English is widely spoken in tourist regions, knowing a few simple French words like "Bonjour" (hello), "Merci" (thank you), "S'il vous plaît" (please), and "Parlez-vous Anglais?" (Do you speak English?) may go a long way. A little effort on your part demonstrates respect for the local culture and can improve your encounters with Parisians.

Booking Reservations in Advance: Popular restaurants, particularly fine-dining venues, are frequently booked well in advance. To avoid disappointment, book reservations for certain restaurants online or by phone ahead of time.

Considering Dietary Restrictions: French food can be high in meat and dairy. If you have dietary limitations, look for eateries that provide vegetarian, vegan, or gluten-free alternatives. Many Parisian restaurants cater to a variety of dietary preferences.

Packing Light Yet Elegantly: While comfort is important, Parisians also dress elegantly. Pack adaptable attire that can be readily combined and matched to create outfits suitable for both informal cafés and more formal restaurants.

Embracing the Metro System: Paris has a well-developed metro system that is both convenient and economical for getting around the city. Purchase a Paris Visite Pass for unlimited access to public transportation, including the metro, buses, and RER trains.

A Parisian Adventure for All Tastes and Passions

Paris is a metropolis that accommodates everyone's likes and interests. Whether you're a picky eater looking for Michelin-starred experiences or a cultural buff seeking hidden jewels and historical lessons, Paris offers something for everyone. This chapter has provided you with the knowledge and practical advice needed to embark on a memorable Parisian vacation that mixes excellent gastronomic encounters with engaging cultural discoveries.

So pack your bags, embrace your curiosity, and get ready to fall in love with the City of Lights! Best wishes and enjoy your journey! (Have a nice journey and enjoy your food!)

France Awaits: Moving Beyond Paris

France, the home of romance, delicious cuisine, and magnificent scenery, has far more to offer than the busy metropolis of Paris. Beyond the City of Lights, explore the charm of the French countryside, where small villages tucked among rolling hills and vineyards provide a perfect vacation. This chapter will serve as your guide to discovering some of France's most intriguing towns and charming villages, transforming your holiday into an amazing journey into the heart of the French way of life.

Charming Towns & Picturesque Villages: Exploring the French Countryside

Provence, a region in southeastern France bordering the Mediterranean Sea, is a visual and sensory feast. Imagine huge lavender fields blanketing rolling hills in purple, attractive communities situated atop hilltops, and a thriving culinary scene that embraces fresh, seasonal products. Here are some Provençal jewels waiting to be discovered:

Gordes (43°48′09″N, 5°19′24″E) is a picturesque hilltop town that has been named one of "Les Plus Beaux Villages de France" (The Most Beautiful Villages of France), making it a photographer's dream. Wander along small cobblestone alleyways dotted with ochre-colored cottages covered with colorful flower pots, taking in the panoramic views of the Luberon Valley. Don't miss the 17th-century Château de Gordes, a spectacular Renaissance castle that currently serves as a modern art museum.

Roussillon (43°50′22″N, 5°28′22″E)

This is a natural marvel, known as the "Colorado Provençal" owing to its brilliant ochre cliffs in reds, oranges, and yellow. Explore the Ochre Trail, a picturesque route that winds past ochre quarries and colorful cliffs, providing breathtaking views of the surrounding landscape. The hamlet itself is a joy, with exquisite cottages constructed of ochre stone that lend to its distinct character.

Saint-Rémy-de-Provence (43°46′22″N, 4°49′12″E)

This is an ideal destination for art and history enthusiasts. This ancient town is well known for being the asylum where Vincent van Gogh spent his last year of life. Immerse yourself in his artistic universe at the Musée Estrine, which has a permanent display of his works, or go to the Saint-Paul-de-Mausoleum, a former asylum where van Gogh lived and painted some of his most famous paintings. Beyond its artistic significance, Saint-Rémy has a delightful old core with a bustling market square and Romanesque architecture.

The Loire Valley: Fairytale Castles and Picturesque Villages

Step back in time and see the Loire Valley, a UNESCO World Heritage Site known for its concentration of majestic châteaux (castles) that tell stories of French royalty. Dotted along the Loire River and its tributaries, these majestic châteaux provide a look into a bygone period of richness and majesty. But the Loire Valley has more than just castles; lovely villages rich in history and natural beauty round out the picture-perfect setting.

Amboise (47°24'22"N, 0°38'32"E)

This is a charming village located on the Loire River, overshadowed by the impressive Château d'Amboise. This regal palace was formerly a favored home for French rulers such as Charles VIII and Francis I. Explore the luxurious chambers, stroll through the expansive grounds, and climb the castle tower for panoramic views of the Loire Valley. The beautiful town center of Amboise has a lovely mix of shops, cafés, and restaurants where you can soak up the local vibe.

Château de Cheverny (47°30'12"N, 1°29'07"E)

This magnificent château is thought to have inspired Hergé, the creator of Tintin, to construct Marlinspike Castle, Captain Haddock's ancestral home. Explore the beautifully adorned interiors and take a stroll around the wide grounds, which are home to a pack of hunting hounds, a long-standing Cheverny tradition. Cheverny is well-known for its vineyards, which produce renowned Loire Valley wines. Sample several local vintages in a delightful wine cellar and enjoy the aromas of the region.

Loches (47°1′33″N, 0°59′32″E) is a fortified city with a thousand-year history. The towering Château de Loches dominates the skyline, comprising three separate structures: the Romanesque Keep, the Royal City (Cité Royale), and the Collegiate Church of Saint-Ours. Explore the Keep, a powerful medieval fortification with panoramic views, and step inside the luxurious rooms of the Royal City, where French kings once lived. The Collegiate Church of Saint-Ours is a marvel of Romanesque architecture, with beautiful sculptures and stained glass windows. The picturesque town center below the castle is a joy to explore, with its half-timbered homes, small lanes, and bustling market square. Don't miss the Halle aux Grains (Grain Market Hall), a 14th-century timber-framed structure that currently houses a busy market with local goods and handcrafted crafts.

Beyond the Featured Gems: Exploring Off-the-Beaten-Path Villages
France has plenty of wonderful villages waiting to be explored. Here are a few ideas to encourage you to go off the beaten path:

Eze, located at 43°43′43″N, 7°27′15″E, is a charming medieval hamlet perched on a cliff top overlooking the Mediterranean Sea. Explore its labyrinthine lanes lined with stone buildings covered with colorful flowers, stop by the Fragonard Perfume Factory to learn about the art of perfume creation, and take in the spectacular views of the Côte d'Azur coastline.

Rocamadour (44°48′44″N, 1°36′44″E) is a pilgrimage destination with shrines constructed into a cliff face in the Dordogne Valley. Ascend the steep road adorned with pilgrim sculptures, tour the different chapels and churches, and take in the spectacular views of the surrounding valley.

Hunspach (48°47'12"N, 7°47'34"E) is located in Alsace, a region bordering Germany. It provides a unique combination of French and German characteristics. Explore the picturesque half-timbered buildings adorned with colorful flower boxes, browse the Christmas shops brimming with festive decorations (Hunspach is recognized as France's Christmas Capital), and try the region's famous Alsatian wines and substantial food.

Experience the French Countryside: Activities and Delights
Beyond the allure of its towns and historical buildings, the French countryside provides a wealth of activities and experiences to immerse yourself in the local way of life.

Wine Tasting in Wine Regions: France has multiple recognized wine regions, each with its own unique grape varietals and wine styles. From the famed vineyards of Bordeaux and Burgundy to the sun-drenched vineyards of Provence and the sparkling wine region of Champagne, take a wine-tasting tour to find your new favorite French wine.

Savoring Local Specialties: French cuisine celebrates fresh, seasonal ingredients. Go beyond the conventional Parisian cuisine and revel in regional delicacies. Enjoy a bouillabaisse, a delicious fish stew, in Marseille, luxurious foie gras (fatty liver) in the Périgord, or a platter of freshly shucked oysters in Brittany.

Exploring Local Markets: Take in the sights, sounds, and fragrances of a French market. Stroll among stands brimming with fresh food, including vivid fruits and vegetables, local cheeses, and cured meats. Pick some picnic goods and pick a picturesque location in the countryside to enjoy a delicious outdoor lunch.

Hiking and Biking in Picturesque Landscapes: The French countryside is a refuge for outdoor enthusiasts. Lace-up your hiking boots or take your bike and experience rolling hills, lush vineyards, and spectacular coastlines. The environment is stunning, and the fresh air energizes.

Plan Your French Countryside Adventure
To guarantee a smooth and pleasurable exploration of the French countryside, consider these suggestions:

Renting an Automobile: The easiest way to go about the quaint villages and scenic countryside is by automobile. This allows you to explore at your own speed while discovering hidden treasures along the way. However, some towns are pedestrian-only, so plan to leave your car outside the village center and explore on foot.

Learning a Few Basic French Words: While English is spoken in some tourist locations, knowing a few basic French words like "Bonjour" (hello), "Merci" (thank you), "S'il vous plaît" (please), and "Parlez-vous Anglais?" (Do you speak English?) will help you get by. A little effort on your part demonstrates respect for the local culture and can improve your contacts with French people.

Day Trips to Historic Sites and Cultural Gems

Beyond the intriguing towns and attractive villages, the French countryside is brimming with historical monuments and cultural treasures waiting to be discovered. This section explores several intriguing day trip choices that will take you back in time while expanding your understanding of French history and culture.

Medieval Wonders: Exploring Castles and Fortresses

France has a rich heritage of medieval architecture, as seen by its numerous castles and strongholds. Here are some ideas for a historical day trip:

Mont Saint-Michel, located at 48°38′12″N, 1°30′41″W, is a UNESCO World Heritage Site with amazing views. Mont Saint-Michel, a tidal island with a fortified monastery, appears to emerge from the water. Explore the small cobblestone alleyways lined with old houses, ascend the majestic staircase to the monastery, and take in the stunning views of the surrounding bay.

Mont Saint-Michel

Consider the tides when planning your visit, since access to the island might be limited at high tide.

Discover Carcassonne (43°12′04″N, 2°11′47″E), a walled city from the 13th century. Carcassonne, a UNESCO World Heritage Site, is one of Europe's most intact medieval cities, with a double ring of ramparts, towers, and a gatehouse. Wander over the walls, see the Château Comtal (Count's Castle), and immerse yourself in a bygone age.

Château de Chambord (47°36'48"N, 1°31'44"E)

This is a UNESCO World Heritage Site and one of the biggest castles in the Loire Valley. It is a masterpiece of Renaissance design. This magnificent tower has an incredible double-helix staircase thought to have been inspired by Leonardo da Vinci, as well as over 400 chambers decorated with tapestries and Renaissance artworks. Explore the expansive grounds that surround the château and immerse yourself in the magnificence of this architectural wonder.

Follow in the Footsteps of History: World War Sites and Memorials

France had an important part in both World Wars, and many historical landmarks and memorials honor those who fought and suffered. Here are a few day travel possibilities for history enthusiasts:

On June 6, 1944, the Allied troops landed on the Normandy D-Day Beaches (49°16′41″N, 0°31′43″W), marking a pivotal moment in World War II. Explore the beaches of Omaha and Utah, where men heroically attacked the shoreline. Pay your respects at the Normandy American Cemetery and Memorial, a moving reminder of the sacrifices made during the liberation of France.

The Somme Battlefields (49°50′N, 2°30′E)

There is a haunting reminder of the tragedies of World War I. Explore the trenches and craters that still mark the terrain, pay a visit to the Thiepval Memorial, which bears the names of almost 72,000 lost British and South African troops, and learn more about this horrific struggle.

The Palace of Versailles (48°48′13″N, 2°07′26″E)

This is famed for its sumptuous architecture and grounds, but it plays a key part in French history. This UNESCO World Heritage Site served as the seat of French kings from the 17th to late 18th centuries. Explore the sumptuous State Apartments, marvel at the grandeur of the Hall of Mirrors, and learn about the key events that occurred within these walls, such as the signing of the Treaty of Versailles, which brought World War I to a close.

Exploring Religious and Cultural Centers
France has a rich religious past and a thriving cultural environment. Consider the following possibilities for a day excursion that provides a look into the country's soul:
Montmartre and Sacré-Coeur Basilica (48°53'11"N, 2°20'14"E)

There are must-sees in Paris, noted for their cultural heritage and pleasant atmosphere. Climb the hill and gaze at the Sacré-Coeur Basilica, a gorgeous white Roman Catholic church with panoramic views of the city. Explore the beautiful alleyways dotted with cafés, art galleries, and souvenir stores, taking in the bohemian vibe of this historic Parisian district.

Chartres Cathedral (48°22″N, 1°29′11″E)

This is a UNESCO World Heritage Site and a must-see for anybody interested in art or history. Construction began in the 12th century, and the cathedral is known for its stained glass windows, some of which date back to the 13th century. These stunning windows portray biblical stories and saints, illuminating the cathedral's interior in a rainbow of hues. Admire the elaborate sculptures on the exterior, explore the labyrinth engraved into the cathedral floor, and behold the architectural miracle that is Chartres Cathedral.

The Guggenheim Museum Bilbao in Spain (43°15′22″N, 2°55′12″W)

This provides a unique cultural experience, while not being situated in France. This Frank Gehry-designed modern architectural marvel holds a modern and contemporary art collection that includes works by Picasso, Rothko, and Jeff Koons. The museum itself is a piece of art, with its whirling titanium curves, and Bilbao's bright Guggenheim provides a thrilling contrast to France's old landmarks.

Improve Your Day Trips: Tips and Considerations

To make the most of your historical and cultural day trips in the French countryside, consider the following suggestions:

Purchase a Pass: Many areas provide history passes that allow you to visit various historical sites and museums at a subsidized rate. To save money and time, look into available passes in the region you'll be visiting.

Plan Your Itinerary: Look up the opening hours and probable closing dates of the locations you want to see. Consider travel time when purchasing tickets online, especially for popular attractions.

Dress Comfortably: Many historical places need a lot of walking, so make sure you wear comfortable shoes. Keep the weather in consideration when packing, especially if you are going during the cooler months.

Embrace Local Culture: Try the native food, learn some basic French words, and interact with the people. These tiny gestures will improve your experience and build a stronger connection to the locations you visit.

Beyond the Suggested Itineraries:
France has a plethora of historical landmarks and cultural wonders waiting to be found. This chapter has given you a beginning point for your investigation, but keep in mind that it is only a small sample of the tremendous treasures that the French countryside offers. Beyond the suggested itineraries, explore the locations that tickle your interest and construct your own one-of-a-kind French historical and cultural trip.

Conclusion

A Fairytale Farewell: Memories That Will Last a Lifetime

As you near the end of this chapter on traveling outside Paris, a bittersweet sense may linger. Exploring picturesque villages and historical buildings is exciting, but it's also a reminder that your French journey is almost over. But don't worry, since the memories you've made will stay with you long after you return home.

The sweeping lavender fields of Provence, the stately châteaux of the Loire Valley, and the spectacular vistas from a medieval hilltop town are just a few of the riches that the French countryside offers. Beyond the looks, it's the experiences that matter. Savoring a beautiful dinner made with fresh, seasonal ingredients, enjoying a glass of wine with newfound friends, or simply taking in the beauty of a local market - these experiences weave the tapestry of your French vacation.

France has a way of capturing the hearts of her tourists. Maybe it's the romanticism in the air, the rich history revealed by ancient stones, or the kindness and friendliness of the French. Whatever the cause, France makes an unforgettable impression, prompting a desire to return and explore further.

This chapter has acted as a guide, but the true voyage of discovery awaits. Pack your suitcases with a feeling of adventure, wanderlust, and a willingness to try new things. France awaits, eager to reveal its charm and create memories that last a lifetime.

A Few Final Tips:
As you finish your preparations, consider these parting words to guarantee a seamless and wonderful experience:

Learn a Few Essential Words: While English is spoken in some tourist locations, a few simple French words such as "Bonjour" (hello), "Merci" (thank you), "Au revoir" (goodbye), and "S'il vous plaît" (please) will get you far. A little effort demonstrates respect for the local culture and can improve your contact with French people.

Embrace the Unexpected: Unplanned adventures may often be the most memorable. Be open to diversions, unexpected discoveries, and hidden treasures along the route.

Travel Slowly and Savor the Moment: Resist the impulse to pack too much into your agenda. Slow down, enjoy the local ambiance, and connect with the places you visit. France is best enjoyed at a slow pace, so you can truly immerse yourself in its beauty.

Good luck and safe travels! (Have a wonderful journey and good luck!) May your French experience be full of fun, exploration, and treasured memories that will last a lifetime.

Tips for Returning Guests: Planning Your Next Magical Adventure

Ah, France! The nation of wonderful food, stunning vistas, and fascinating history has captured your heart, and you long to return. Welcome return, beloved wanderer. This section is specifically designed for you, the returning adventurer looking to dig further into the wonder of France.

Since you've previously seen the classic attractions of Paris and may have even journeyed beyond the city on your last trip, this book concentrates on creating a one-of-a-kind and personalized itinerary for your return. Here are some suggestions to start your planning ideas flowing:

Explore a New Region:
France has a rich patchwork of regions, each with its own particular flavor. Did the undulating lavender fields and colorful culture of Provence entice you? Perhaps venture farther into the south to discover the lovely villages of the Dordogne Valley or the breathtaking beaches of the French

Riviera. Alternatively, if the magnificence of the Loire Valley châteaux has left you speechless, drive west to Brittany, a country rich in Celtic history and with spectacular coasts.

Seek out Off-the-Beaten-Path Gems
France is full of hidden treasures waiting to be uncovered. Explore lovely villages situated among rolling hills or attractive towns along lesser-known canals, rather than sticking to the well-trodden tourist trail. Research area festivals and cultural events taking place during your stay. Accept the opportunity to immerse yourself in the true French way of life and interact with local populations.

Theme your Trip Around Your Passions
Do you have a special interest in French wines? Plan a wine-tasting trip in a well-known wine area, such as Bordeaux, Burgundy, or Champagne. Are you a history buff? Customize your itinerary to include historical places relevant to your region of interest, such as medieval castles and Roman ruins. France caters to a range of interests, so use yours as a guide to create an amazing experience.

Embrace Slow Travel

Instead of hurrying from one site to the next, try adopting the philosophy of leisurely travel. Choose a pleasant base in a place that appeals to you and spend your days visiting the nearby villages, markets, and hidden jewels. Enjoy leisurely lunches at local cafés, strike up talks with merchants, and genuinely connect with the flow of life in a certain location.

Learn Some New French phrases:

While English is spoken in certain tourist destinations, brushing up on your French may go a long way. Focus on ordinary language such as ordering meals, asking for directions, and expressing appreciation. The locals will appreciate your efforts, and your trip will go even more smoothly.

Travel in the Shoulder Seasons:

To escape the peak summer crowds, consider traveling during the shoulder seasons, which are spring and fall. The weather is frequently good, lodging costs are lower, and major sights are less packed, resulting in a more relaxing and personal experience.

Embrace Serendipity

Allow for some improvisation in your agenda. Be open to unexpected diversions, suggestions from friendly locals, and hidden jewels you discover along the road. Unplanned discoveries can lead to some of the most unforgettable experiences.

Pack Light and Versatile

As you learned from your previous trip, pack light and adaptable clothing that can be readily combined and matched to create acceptable ensembles for various circumstances. Comfortable shoes are required for seeing picturesque villages and historical places on foot.

Document Your Memories:
Capture the thrill of your French vacation with photographs, films, or even a travel blog. These artifacts will allow you to recollect those wonderful moments long after you return home.

Most essential, embrace the French joie de vivre (the joy of living). Enjoy the great food, see the beauty of the scenery, and immerse yourself in the vibrant culture. France has so much to offer, and with these suggestions, you'll be well on your way to organizing a wonderfully magical return trip.

Have a safe journey and return soon! (Have a wonderful vacation and return soon!)

Glossary

While English is extensively spoken at Disneyland Paris, learning a few simple French words will help you enjoy your visit and impress the park's cast members. Here are a few crucial phrases to remember:

Greetings and Farewell:
Bonjour (bon-zhoor): Good day
Salut: Hello (casual).
Bon soir (bon-swahr): Good evening.
Merci (mehr-see): Thank you!
S'il vous plaît (see voo play)
Au revoir (oh reh-vwar) means goodbye.
Enchanté(e) (ahn-shahn-tay/tay): Nice to meet you.
Basic Needs:

Excusez-moi (ehs-koo-zay mwah).
Where are the toilets? (oo sont lay twah-let): Where are the restrooms?
Je voudrais... (Zhuh Voo-Dray): I'd want...
How much does this cost? (combien sah Koot): How much will this cost?
I do not comprehend.

Can you speak slower? (poo-vay voo par-lay polo lent-mah): Could you please talk slowly?
Disneyland-Specific Phrases:

I have a FastPass (jay fahst-pah).
Is this for a single rider? Does this ride feature a single-rider line?
Where is the show? (oo suh troov luh spek-takl).
What is the upcoming show? What's the next show?
I would like to meet Mickey.
Expressing gratitude:

It was magical! Say-tay mah-cheek: That was amazing!
Thank you for the unforgettable day! Thank you for a fantastic day!
We were amused! (On Suh Byan Ah-myoo-zay): We had a fantastic time!
Bonus Phrases:

Oui (Wee): Yes.
Non: No.
Have a pleasant day!

Thank you very much!
Remember, pronunciation is essential! Do not be scared to practice your French, even if it isn't flawless. The CMs will appreciate your efforts and may even offer you a "Bonjour" or "Merci" in return!

Your honest review can make a huge difference in increasing the visibility of this book. Please take a moment to share your thoughts and help others discover this valuable resource.

Printed in Great Britain
by Amazon